Matt Burden not only does a great job walking us through the history of missionary work found in the Church Fathers, but he also nicely connects the history to our present need to be a missional people. This book is not only theologically sound and informative but allows the current missionary-minded Christian to connect to the past efforts of the men and women who transformed the world by living the present Kingdom of Christ in their daily lives. I highly recommend this book to every Christian who takes the command to preach the Gospel always seriously.

FATHER DOMINICK D. HANKLE, PhD
Professor of Psychology, Regent University

Every lasting enterprise needs a profound "why." This includes God's global mission enterprise throughout the millennia, as well as our own personal mission enterprise during our lifespan. Matt Burden has done us all the service of identifying the "why" of the early church—her missionary motivations. Yes, missionary motivations in the plural, because they were much more diverse than those commonly referred to today in evangelicalism, which are usually the Great Commission, love for the lost, and the glory of God. Matt has done meticulous work, and he presents it with ease of access and great clarity. Whether you benefit from deepening your own motivation for your personal involvement in missions or desire to deepen the motivation of those you lead or those you want to mobilize—you will find Matt's volume a gold mine.

EMANUEL PRINZ (DMin, PhD Candidate)
Mission Researcher and Author, *Movement Catalysts*

Here is a serious and revealing look at the history and theology of the early centuries of Christian expansion that can powerfully impact and shape the church's mission today. My four decades of local congregation, frontline missions, and classroom experience convince me that we must dig deeper in our study of the past. Burden is scholarly yet efficient and very approachable in his writing, and he clearly summarizes and applies what he discovers. Church leaders, students, and missionaries in preparation must grab and devour this book. If I were back in the classroom, it would be required reading and a platform for healthy and prayerful discussion. What a wonderful addition to some of the great writers and thinkers in mission history, theology, and practice! I am so thankful for its potential with the Spirit's backing to motivate the church live out the reign of Christ today.

PAUL W. SHEA, DMiss
Emeritus Professor, Missions and Intercultural Studies, Houghton University
Missionary in Sierra Leone, W. Africa with Wesleyan Global Partners

I recently discussed with an experienced Japanese missionary possible reasons why the church has failed to impact this society. It prepared me to read this book. I found it to be an enjoyable, stimulating, refreshing, and instructive read. It is scholarly but would appeal to many pastors and lay people.

It is a must-read contribution to the debate about why the church is failing to impact many societies in today's world. Matt examines some of the possible, diverse reasons for the early amazing expansion of the early church into Europe, India, Asia, and China. At the same time it reflects upon how the contemporary church might employ them sensitively and contextually.

Rev. Roger Tucker, PhD
Emeritus Minister, United Presbyterian Church in Southern Africa
Research Fellow, Department of Practical Theology, University of the Free State

Rarely do I begin making a list of people to whom I'd recommend a book … before I've even finished reading the first chapter. But such was the case with Matthew Burden's *Missionary Motivations*, a fascinating study of mission motivation in the early church. Where some authors might scratch the surface or succumb to guesswork when the historical data is sometimes sparse, Burden digs out the gold. His discoveries, the found wisdom, and his own insights offer a valuable study that is theologically and practically applicable today. The book's rich insights from ancient church history can help forge the missional identity of the future. Matthew Burden has made a sizable and very readable contribution to historical mission studies. *Missionary Motivations* offers a grand challenge to those willing to reflect on the past and act with intentionality in today's church and mission contexts.

Susan Van Wynen, PhD
Strategy Consultant and Leadership Team Member, Wycliffe Global Alliance

MISSIONARY MOTIVATIONS
Challenges from the Early Church

Matthew Burden

Available at missionbooks.org

Missionary Motivations: Challenges from the Early Church

© 2023 by Matthew Burden. All Rights Reserved.

No part of this book may be reproduced, stored in a retrieval system, or transmitted in any form or by any means—electronic, mechanical, photocopy, recording, or otherwise—without prior written permission from the publisher, except brief quotations used in connection with reviews in magazines or newspapers. For permission, email permissions@wclbooks.com. For corrections, email editor@wclbooks.com.

Scripture quotations are from the ESV® Bible (The Holy Bible, English Standard Version®), Copyright © 2001 by Crossway, a publishing ministry of Good News Publishers. Used by permission. All rights reserved.

Published by William Carey Publishing
10 W. Dry Creek Cir
Littleton, CO 80120 | www.missionbooks.org

William Carey Publishing is a ministry of Frontier Ventures
Pasadena, CA | www.frontierventures.org

Cover and Interior Designer: Mike Riester
Cover image by Svetlana Vorotniak, iStock.com

ISBNs: 978-1-64508-475-4 (paperback)
           978-1-64508-477-8 (epub)

Printed Worldwide

27 26 25 24 23   2 3 4 5 6   IN

Library of Congress Control Number: 2023933107

Contents

Introduction	vii
Chapter 1 The Shape of Early Christian Mission	1
Chapter 2 Miracles and Martyrdoms: Expansion within the Roman Empire	15
Chapter 3 Empires and Trade Routes: Expansion to the East	35
Chapter 4 The Call of the Desert: Expansion to the South	47
Chapter 5 Barbarian Gospel: Expansion in Central Europe	61
Chapter 6 The Distant Islands Shall Rejoice: Expansion in Northern Europe	75
Chapter 7 The Mission of the Kingdom: Communal Aspects of Missionary Motivation	89
Chapter 8 Emissaries of the King: Individual Aspects of Missionary Motivation	101
Chapter 9 Mission in the Spirit of Early Christianity	113
Bibliography	126
Index	129

Introduction

We offer earnest prayers ... for all people everywhere.
—Justin Martyr, *First Apology* 1.65

I grew up as the son of evangelical missionaries, serving with Wycliffe Bible Translators first in Brazil and later at a Wycliffe training camp in Texas. The idea of Christian mission "for all people everywhere" was a formative influence on my young worldview. One of my most powerful early memories comes from watching my father give missionary presentations in supporting churches when we were back on home assignment. Taking a ream of old-style computer paper (the kind that was connected end-to-end along perforated edges), he would flip through the ream as he spoke, sending a cascade of paper over the front of the pulpit until it formed a billowing mass on the floor in front of the church stage.

That ream of paper, though, wasn't blank. It was filled with text, an immense list of all the people groups in the world who had yet to receive the Bible in their own language. It was an illustration of the scale of the task that lay before us, and whatever the impression it made on the rest of the audience, it made a deep impression on me. The point was clear: there were a lot of people still in need of access to Scripture. There was an underlying premise to the exercise, too, one that didn't even need to be explained to me: it was our duty, as the church of Jesus Christ, to bring the message of his gospel to a waiting world.

But why was this our duty? What, exactly, was our motivation for going out as missionaries? To many people, the question seems almost too obvious to be worth asking. The answers look clear, at least to those of us who grew up in the milieu of Protestant Christianity after the "Great Century" of missions in the 1800s and the renewed waves of the 1900s. If you had asked me about missionary motivations as I watched my father flip a massive list of unreached people groups over the pulpit, I would probably have given you two answers. First, we go out to bear the gospel because that is what Jesus commanded us to do. In the Great Commission of Matthew 28:18–20, his instructions are clear and compelling: "Go therefore and make disciples of all nations" (v. 19).

Second, we go out of concern for the welfare of all those people who have not yet heard the gospel. As Paul says in Romans 10:14, "How then will they call on him in whom they have not believed? And how are they to believe in him of whom they have never heard? And how are they to hear without someone preaching?" Later, as I studied missiology in college,

I could have added more reasons as well, answers which encompassed not only the message of the gospel but the whole work of the kingdom of God. Even so, those answers still came down to just a couple motivating principles: we engage upon these labors out of obedience to our Lord's command and out of sincere compassion for the people of the world.

I was soon to discover, however, that these answers were not as clear and obvious as I had assumed. In fact, vast swathes of church history—including some historical missionary movements—had not articulated those motivating factors at all. Rather, the writers and missionaries of earlier eras of the faith seemed to be operating on a somewhat different theological wavelength, and it resulted in different answers to the question of missionary motivation. These answers often appeared as natural and obvious to them as mine were to me, but, strangely enough, they were different answers. I do not mean to say that my earlier answers for missionary motivation had been wrong. They still strike me as obvious and compelling. But it may be the case that there are also other answers, answers which some of us may not have considered, answers compelling enough to broaden our understanding and inspire fresh efforts for the work of the kingdom. This book tells the story of those complementary answers, as they emerged from the experiences of the first centuries of Christian expansion.

> *It may be the case that there are answers compelling enough to broaden our understanding and inspire fresh efforts for the work of the kingdom.*

It was the study of patristics that led me to this exploration of missionary motivations. Beginning in seminary, I launched on a personal program to read as much and as many of the works of the early church fathers as I could. I knew that Christianity had expanded rapidly in its earliest centuries, both within the Roman Empire and beyond. It struck me as strange, then, that my assumptions regarding missionary motivations rarely, if ever, appeared in those sources, even amid a period of significant expansion. So I undertook a research thesis on the topic as an independent study, and later added postgraduate and doctoral studies in history and theology, in order to better understand the contours of missiological thought in other periods of church history.

The focus of my scholarly work centers on historical missiology, an attempt to understand the missiological thinking of other eras in the life of the church. Historical missiology, as a discipline, is analogous to the position held by historical theology. Historical theology sits between systematic theology and church history, attempting to describe how the theology of earlier periods of Christianity would have been understood and articulated. Similarly, historical missiology is a subject that sits between missiology and the history of mission, and it seeks to describe the way that earlier periods understood and articulated their principles of missiology. Such an enterprise is difficult, because most earlier periods of Christianity simply did not produce systematic treatments of their missiological thought, but reasonable reconstructions can be built from the evidence that remains.

While the story of early Christian missions has been told and studied many times, it is usually with an aim toward historical and practical understandings, rather than toward theological concerns. This study aims to help fill that gap by opening a window on the way that Christians in the early centuries of our faith thought about the task of global mission. In short, it seeks to expand our understanding of the history of mission with a theological element, by exploring the theologies of mission which undergirded the spread of the Christian gospel in earlier periods. It also seeks to expand our understanding of patristic theology. Theological studies in the early centuries of Christian thought tend to focus on doctrinal issues of Trinitarian theology, Christology, and soteriology, and only rarely, if ever, on the development of missiological ideas. This study aims to help fill that gap, if only in a small and introductory way.

The question of missionary motivations is not an easy one to uncover by historical research, for the very reason that it was often simply assumed by the writers of primary sources. In the same way that I felt my reasons for missionary motivation were so clear and obvious to hardly necessitate explication, writers in ancient and early medieval Christianity only rarely saw the need of explaining the underlying motivations of their subject matter. In many cases, the sources simply do not speak directly or with clarity regarding missiological ideas, and so the data must be pieced together from a reasonable assessment of the sources' information regarding means, methods, and mission narratives.

Further, the scope of this project sweeps across multiple centuries and cultures, and, as one might expect, not all of them had precisely the same ways of thinking about the missionary call of Christian faith or the process of conversion. As the anthropologist Peter Wells notes, "Examining the process of conversion to Christianity is complex and difficult, because no single source of information provides us with a consistent picture of the changing situation."[1] The process of discerning such things, then, is something akin

---
1 Wells, *Barbarians to Angels*, 172.

to assembling a giant mosaic: It requires the work of placing down enough pieces of data from historical movements and evangelistic practices to be able to see the emerging shape of the whole picture. Only then can we build a sense from our written sources as to what the probable motivations of missionary labors were within the context of earlier ages of our faith. The reconstruction provided in this study is just that: a reconstruction. It seeks to articulate theological principles that were quite often unconscious and unarticulated by those who held them, but even so, the pattern of their words and deeds provides a window into framing and understanding at least some of these hidden motivations.

This book is structured in two parts, following some introductory theological considerations in chapter 1. First, it presents a broad survey of evangelistic practices, missionary movements, and references to missiological ideas from the source materials of various times and places in early Christianity (chs. 2–5). This historical survey section will examine Christian expansion within the territories of the Roman Empire (ch. 2), then devote chapters to its expansion to the east (ch. 3), south (ch. 4), and north (chs. 5 and 6). The time period in view runs from the end of the first century into the eighth, which encompasses the patristic period. This chronological range also includes the entire Christian experience through the periods of classical antiquity and late antiquity, the latter of which is usually marked with an endpoint around the mid-eighth century.

Second, this book will explain some of the main theological contours of early Christianity's missiological thinking (chs. 7–9). Again, because of the temporal and geographical scope of this book, these sections will necessarily be an overview and a synthesis of multiple perspectives. The main missiological themes which I highlight are as follows: a motivation based in the theology of Christ's present reign, which expresses itself in several communally oriented aspects of mission practice (ch. 7); in the theology of human identity and the Christian's restored offices in Christ, which brings some individually oriented aspects to bear (ch. 8); and in the development of missional church cultures in various times and places throughout Christianity's early periods, which offers insights to today's Christian who seeks to do mission in the spirit of early Christianity (ch. 9).

A brief note on terminology before we begin: the history of Christian expansion in the early centuries can be difficult to trace, and it does not always align itself within conventional definitions of "evangelism" and "mission." This book will use both terms somewhat interchangeably, although with distinctions. Their main commonality is that both terms relate a sense of *intentionality*, in which a Christian makes a decision to be engaged in active outreach, and then follows through with it. "Evangelism" will refer mostly to passing on the substance of the gospel message, but with distinctions between active and passive modes (of which chapter 2 will have more to say). "Mission" often includes a sense of the dissemination of the faith across cultural, national, ethnic, or linguistic boundaries, but it also serves as an overarching term for the church's participation in God's work in the world. Again, the most important sense of each term, for the purposes of this book, is that they relate a sense of intentionality on the part of the Christian.

While the theological context of missionary motivations constitutes this book's primary concern, it also seeks to be inspirational, and, I hope, practical. My desire is not only to help readers understand the mindset of the early Christian centuries better, but, if possible, to apply some of those understandings to the contemporary missional life of the church. This book is an effort to "hear what the Spirit says to the churches" (Rev 2–3)—that is, to tune our ears to what the Holy Spirit was saying to our forerunners in their missional context, and to learn how to better undertake the works to which God calls us here and now. By listening to the reflections which emerge from earlier ages of Christian expansion, we may find insight to instruct and inspire us for labors yet to come.

> *By listening to the reflections which emerge from earlier ages of Christian expansion, we may find insight to instruct and inspire us for labors yet to come.*

Chapter 1
The Shape of Early Christian Mission

The story of Christianity's early rise is remarkable. No one who lived in the Roman world when Augustus Caesar reigned could have predicted that within three centuries, the pagan underpinnings of the empire would be in a state of catastrophic collapse, replaced by the rapid advance of an obscure sect from the backwaters of Palestine. While it's true that exposure to new or different systems of belief happened regularly in ancient Rome, those new systems were usually incorporated into the existing pagan structure without much trouble. But in Christianity, a new movement had broken out upon the world, one with universal and exclusive claims, before which all the centuries-long traditions of Greco-Roman paganism shattered with startling suddenness. It wasn't just the Roman world, either—within three centuries after Christ, the new faith was sweeping across the vast Asian continent to the east and making inroads deep into Africa and northern Europe. These gains would go on to be magnified and multiplied, time and time again, over the centuries that followed.

One of the most striking elements of this growth was its originality. The Mediterranean world had never seen something like this. As a general rule, religion in the ancient Mediterranean was a pluralistic affair. Each nation had its own faith, its own gods, and while the nations' gods were thought occasionally to go to war with one another, most religious systems were not exclusive. This was particularly true of the Roman mindset, which accepted the notion that while they had their own pantheon of gods, other places might have other gods (or local variations of the Romans' own gods, called by other names). A Roman who found himself in a foreign land would often just add that place's native gods to his own pious observances, at least while he remained in that area.

But a faith which claimed the prerogative of total and exclusive allegiance—not only over its own people, but over all people—was something wildly new. While a few faiths, like Second Temple Judaism, held truth-claims which applied to all people, such faiths did not actively seek the recognition of those truth-claims from everyone else. Jews believed there was only one God and thought the Romans' polytheism false, but they did not necessarily expect all Romans to come to a recognition of that truth. They wrote against idolatry and welcomed Gentile God-fearers, but never engaged in the sort of sustained outreach which characterized Christianity's rapid ascent.

Christianity was unique, and it accomplished something which had not yet been seen in the history of Mediterranean religion.

What caused this dramatic onward surge in Christianity's rise? At a fundamental level, it must have been driven by the simple, practical reality of the gospel's proclamation, either by evangelists or ordinary Christians, as the witness of their lives gave them opportunity to share their faith. Seen in its broad outlines, it looks like a marvelous success story in evangelism, mission, and personal witness. Many modern Christians—particularly those from an evangelical background, who put great emphasis on the dissemination of the faith as a foundational part of the Christian life—feel very much at home with the story of early Christianity.

> *Christianity was unique, and it accomplished something which had not yet been seen in the history of Mediterranean religion.*

But dig a little deeper, and that feeling fades. There is a certain dissonance that arises between the way we think about the need for evangelism and mission, and the way that early Christians appear to have thought about it. To get a sense of that dissonance, consider the following:

- The Great Commission texts from Matthew, Acts, and the long ending of Mark are largely absent from the many scriptural references in the texts of the post-apostolic centuries. Strangely enough, those verses appear not to have loomed large in the early church's mindset.
- While the spread of Christianity is undeniable during those early centuries, the actual means of that spread are often difficult to piece together from historical sources. The dissemination of the faith is not center stage in most sources.
- Where early Christian sources do speak about the spread of the Christian faith, they rarely put the matter in terms familiar to modern Christians, still less to evangelical Christians. There is seldom any appeal to obedience to biblical commands like the Great Commission, nor does one often find references to a sense of concern for the salvation or spiritual wellbeing of nonbelievers.

What motivated the spread of Christianity if it wasn't a matter of biblical obedience or concern for others? We can't always know for sure, but we can make some plausible guesses from the things the early sources do talk about.

While this book examines Christianity in the periods after the apostolic age (with just a couple of exceptions), it is worth noting that some interesting features are present in the New Testament itself. The disciples, for their part, appear to be motivated by obedience to Christ's command. And Paul, when he describes his own missionary calling as an apostle to the Gentiles, evinces a clear sense of concern for nonbelievers (see, for example, Rom 10:14–17). There are also other motivations at play in the New Testament—in Paul's thought, not least the idea that his missionary labors win for him affirmation from the Lord (as in 2 Tim 4:7–8).

Note, however, that the New Testament does not direct much counsel regarding evangelism or missionary labors to anyone other than the apostles themselves. The epistles are largely concerned with giving practical counsel to ordinary Christians regarding the life of faith, and yet very little of these practical sections are concerned with missional practices beyond the general appeal of living in holiness.

From the way that post-apostolic Christians dealt with evangelism and missions in their sources, it seems that they picked up on this distinction between the apostles and other Christians. Judging from those texts, the generations of Christians who followed the apostles thought that Paul's missionary sentiments, part and parcel as they were of his calling as an apostle to the Gentiles, did not necessarily extend or apply to anyone beyond the apostle himself. Similarly, there appears to have been a general feeling that the Great Commission had been given to the disciples and their generation, and that the disciples had fulfilled it (at least in an incipient way). Far from being a continuing obligation of all Christians, the Great Commission was interpreted as a *fait accompli*, as illustrated in the following passage from the monastic writer Cyril of Scythopolis (sixth century):

> Accordingly, when [Jesus] sent out his disciples for the salvation of our race, he said, "Go and teach all nations, baptizing them in the name of the Father and of the Son and of the Holy Spirit." On receiving this teaching, they sped through the whole world to proclaim piety by both word and deed … . This is why the knowledge of God has risen upon the world; … this is why from all nations flocks of holy martyrs have sprung up … . (*Lives of the Monks of Palestine* 7.15–8.1)

Early Christianity does not show a significant tendency toward applying either the Great Commission or Paul's missionary sentiments to anyone beyond the apostolic generation. Nevertheless, it was a profoundly missional age. The only puzzling thing is that we don't always know how early Christianity understood or expressed its missional impulses. As Alan Kreider notes, "According to the evidence at our disposal, the expansion of the churches was not organized, the product of a mission program; it simply happened."[1] The staggering growth of Christianity across its first centuries is testimony that there remained a driving force of evangelism and mission working in the background. It may not have grounded itself primarily in the Great Commission, nor in statements of concern for the lost, but it must have been there, or else the rise of the Christian faith would be historically inexplicable.

There were passive means of evangelism, to be sure—the witness of daily lives lived in love and kindness, of public displays of faith and humility, which no doubt drew many to the faith—but there were also active means of evangelism at work. We have anecdotal evidence from the histories and hagiographies of early Christianity that there were people actively engaged in spreading the message of Christ to those who had never heard it before. How would the protagonists of those stories articulate their reasons for going? What were the motivating factors behind such acts? When Christians served as witnesses to the gospel of their Lord, whether to their own neighbors or to a new and distant land, what exactly were the ideas that drove such behavior? This book will seek to provide answers to those questions.

The Reign of Christ

When one reads across the spectrum of early Christianity, there emerges a picture of a young and vibrant faith which believes itself to be the earthly representation of a heavenly reality, a signpost of the way that God was breaking into the life of the world. There was an overriding conviction that an entirely new stage of history had begun, a glorious age of Christ the Priest-King's reign, and that the Christian church constituted the embassy outposts of that advancing reign, expanding its influence until it touched the very ends of the earth. It was a vision of a global Christian community, united not just in its passion for saving souls for a future heavenly existence, but for establishing churches which manifested the present reality of heaven's irruption into history.

This vision of Christian expansion is deeply rooted in the original proclamation of Jesus and the disciples as recorded in the Gospels: "the good news of the kingdom of God." The word translated as "kingdom" here, *basileia*, could more properly be rendered as "reign." Everything centered on the revelation of the reign of God through Christ Jesus, revealed in the events of his life, death, resurrection, and ascension. Christians held the conviction that their master Jesus now participated in the reign of God, thus

---
[1] Kreider, *Patient Ferment*, 9.

making it, at the same time, the reign of the messianic king.[2] It was this idea of the present reign of Jesus, demonstrated and sealed in his earthly ministry, which drove much of the missional expansion of the early church.

To understand how this worked, we need to spend some time teasing out exactly what early Christians understood regarding this idea of the reign of Christ. For many modern western Christians, the proclamation of "the kingdom of God" seems like a puzzling notion, perhaps just a vague metaphor of the salvation that would be offered through Jesus. We are so inclined to hear the message of the gospel through the lens of its later applications, focusing on the individual need for the forgiveness of sins, that we've lost some of the scope and grandeur of Jesus's initial proclamation.

For the past century and a half, New Testament scholars have noted just how different the Protestant articulation of the gospel is when compared to the message preached by Jesus. Somehow, a message of the reign of God was transmuted into a gospel about individual salvation through the forgiveness of personal sins. The blame for this transition is often laid at the feet of the apostle Paul, who is accused by the revisionist wing of biblical scholarship of inventing a whole new kind of Christianity than what Jesus intended. Such a view, however, is deeply short-sighted. Many scholars are now realizing that Paul's message was intertwined with Jesus's proclamation of the kingdom, and that the classic idea of salvation by faith alone, as derived from his epistles, ought probably to be understood more in the sense of faith as *allegiance* rather than as simply *intellectual assent*—and allegiance is a kingdom idea.

> *It was this idea of the present reign of Jesus, demonstrated and sealed in his earthly ministry, which drove much of the missional expansion of the early church.*

Rather than saying that Paul took Christianity in a whole different direction, it would be better to say that Paul explained Jesus's gospel in its applications to the expansion of the faith from Jewish to Gentile circles. The western tradition, long enmeshed in an individualist rather than a communal culture, took Paul's applications and understood them in the context of each individual's life: salvation thus becoming a matter of the personal forgiveness of sins. This doesn't mean that western Christians have been reading Paul wrong, any more than Paul was reading Jesus wrong. My personal salvation certainly is a matter of God's grace forgiving my sins

---
2 See Dunn, *Did the First Christians?*, 103.

through the sacrifice of Christ. But this dynamic does suggest that one set of applications of the gospel (admittedly, a crucial and nonnegotiable set) came to stand, eventually, for the whole gospel. Those applications were not wrong, but it still behooves us to look back and see what might have been missed along the way as an individualized aspect of the gospel was prioritized over other aspects.

What, then, did Jesus mean when he came proclaiming that "the reign of God" was at hand? In the context of his audience, raised in Second Temple Judaism's wild and desperate whirl of expectations for the messianic age and the fulfillment of everything God had been doing through the history of the Jewish people, the proclamation of God's reign would have struck at least two significant chords. First, it would have struck a chord which spoke of the final establishment of God's righteousness in all the world through the promised Messiah's kingship, and second, a chord which reminded them of the abiding presence of God himself.

Jesus's proclamation of the reign of God likely would have made his audience's mind leap forward, envisioning the promised eschatological future of the Last Day, when the Messiah would take up his throne, the nations be judged, and the righteousness of God established over all creation. It should be underscored that this was presented as *good news*. Nowadays, many Christians think about prophecies of the Last Day as something foreboding, even terrifying. While the grim realities of judgment certainly could be a central feature of those prophecies, their Old Testament context more often addressed them in a tenor of hope—the world was thoroughly broken and wicked, and it needed the hand of a good and righteous Judge to set everything right again. The expectations of the Last Day were fused to a brilliantly hopeward vision of the future, in which God would make all things well. Further, one of the central expectations of the messianic age—based on the prophecies of the Last Day—was that under the Messiah, the nations would be brought back into worshipful submission to the God of Israel. Jesus proclaims all this as good news: the promised restoration is nearly upon us, at hand and accessible even now in the person of the Messiah.

> *One of the central expectations of the messianic age ... was that under the Messiah, the nations would be brought back into worshipful submission to the God of Israel.*

His proclamation of the reign of God would have also led his audience to think about the past, striking a chord of God's abiding presence in the temple. The early traditions of Israel's monarchy admitted that they were a concession to the weakness of God's covenant people. They ought to have been content to live under God as their king, but they weren't, so God permitted them to have earthly kings. There was one place, however, where the idea of the reign of God continued to be perpetually present: in the temple's Holy of Holies. The ark of the covenant, sitting there in the inner sanctum, is presented throughout Scripture as the footstool of the throne of God, and the representations of cherubim (thought to be throne-angels in Jewish tradition) reinforce the notion that the Holy of Holies was directly connected to the heavenly courts. The psalms often draw on temple imagery when they present the heavenly reign of God, and so it is likely that Jesus's audience would have heard his message of "the reign of God" in terms of temple theology.

What would it mean, then, to say that "the kingdom of God is at hand"? One thing it might mean is that the abiding presence of God himself, heretofore enclosed in a single room in Jerusalem's temple, is now present and accessible in the person of Jesus. The reign of God is set loose, breaking in upon the world and its kingdoms, on the move in the ministry of the Messiah. Now the whole world will become the temple of the presence of God, as his reign is made manifest to the ends of the earth. This, indeed, is exactly what the prophets foretold: "For the earth will be filled with the knowledge of the glory of the LORD as the waters cover the sea" (Hab 2:14; Isa 11:9). The experience of the glory of the Lord—the *shekinah* radiance of his presence—will fill the whole earth, as God's temple-reign becomes his universal reign through the work of the Messiah.

To put it simply, the message of "the kingdom of God" would have been heard not just as a call to personal salvation, but as the announcement that the long-awaited age of God's restoration had broken upon humanity, and that it would be made manifest in the coronation, enthronement, and reign of the great Messiah-king. The call of the gospel was, in the words of N. T. Wright, "an inaugurated eschatological message"—in short, that the coming age had already begun to appear through the work of the Messiah, and a way had been opened to experience the life of the kingdom even now.[3]

Christians believed that their community—the church, represented in thousands of local instantiations—was the embassy of the Messiah's heavenly reign, symbolizing, in an anticipatory way, the kingdom's in-breaking upon the world. The church was not the kingdom in all its fullness, for that was still to come, but it was a bridge upon the way to the kingdom's fullness.

---

3 Wright, *How God Became King*, 37.

The *Odes of Solomon* (the earliest Christian hymnbook) uses kingdom-language to refer to the church: "Upon [Thy rock] Thou hast built Thy kingdom, and it became the dwelling-place of the holy ones" (22.11–12). Early Christians did not hold a realized eschatology, but they did tend to hold a high ecclesiology, in which the church existed as an eschatological sign of the in-breaking kingdom of God. It was a living portent, standing in the midst of human societies, pointing straight to what God was doing in their midst through the advancing reign of the Messiah.

The Messianic Priest-King

If the early church's understanding was grounded in expectations of the messianic reign, what exactly did that mean? What was their vision of the Messiah? What were the expectations of his reign? According to various traditions of Second Temple Judaism, the Messiah was expected to be both a royal and a priestly figure.[4] He was expected to fulfil the types presented by figures throughout the history of Israel, centering especially on David and Melchizedek. Discernible in Old Testament passages like Psalm 110 and the book of Zechariah, as well as in intertestamental texts like the Melchizedek document from the Dead Sea Scrolls, a vision emerges of a coming messianic leader who is both a king and a priest. The New Testament links each of these roles with Christ's passion narrative and with his subsequent ascension and heavenly enthronement.

The early Christians understood these intertwined roles of king and priest as coming to their fulfillment in the ministry of Jesus Christ, and particularly in the events of his passion.[5] Although Jesus could have claimed the royal office for himself at any point during his ministry, he avoided doing so until his final visit to Jerusalem, when his triumphal entry and clearing of the temple courts asserted his royal prerogatives in no uncertain terms. He was arrested on the charge of claiming kingship and was surrounded by royal regalia on the way to his execution: the crown of thorns, the robe, the mock submission from the soldiers, and the sign placed above his head. To early Christians, all these little symbols, though they were intended as mockery, actually spoke the truth about what was happening. The true king, represented in God's suffering servant, was receiving his coronation rites. Like all good kings were expected to do, Jesus was going out to battle the enemies of his people—sin, death, and Satan—and to shatter their hold over his sovereign possessions.

---

4 Longenecker, *Christology of Early Jewish Christianity*, 65–66.
5 Longenecker, 74.

In equal measure, the events of Jesus's passion spoke of his priestly role. His teaching in Jerusalem's streets, his critique of the corrupt temple priesthood, his institution of a new rite of worship in communion, and his self-offering on the cross all painted a picture of the messianic priest engaged in his mission. The resurrection validates both his kingly and priestly missions: confirming his victory over the enemy powers of sin, death, and Satan, and assuring that needy sinners would not only have a redeeming sacrifice, but a living high priest to present that sacrifice before God on their behalf.

The ascension takes the picture one step further: not only has the priest-king been crowned by his labors, now he rises to his enthronement, endowed with the sovereignty of reigning in the fullness of both intertwining offices. While many modern Christians struggle to explain the ascension beyond a historical event that demonstrates Jesus's present absence, the early Christian witness made the ascension one of the central claims of the gospel proclamation. It appears prominently in all the earliest proclamations of the gospel in Acts, right alongside references to the crucifixion and resurrection. The disciples present it not as a mystery to be explained away, but as proof positive of Jesus's claims. The ascension accounts,

> *The vision of early Christianity was that the king was on the throne and was drawing back together the shattered pieces of his royal endowment.*

which reflect both royal and priestly themes, convince the early Christian community that their rabbi has gone into the heavenly temple-courts to present his sacrifice as the great high priest, and has been granted dominion and authority to reign at the Father's right hand. Jesus's ministry did not end with the ascension; it was merely a transition to a new phase, in which "he must reign until he has put all his enemies under his feet" (1 Cor 15:25).[6]

Viewed in this light, the present age is far more than just a strange hiatus in which we await Jesus's return. It is the opening drama of the messianic age itself. The reign of Christ is active and on the move, claiming the submission of earth's kingdoms to its sovereign sway, expressed in salvation, holiness, and love. In this very age, the prophecies of God's great restoration are already being fulfilled: the nations are streaming up to Zion to worship the God of Israel, and pure sacrifices of praise and thanksgiving are being offered up to him from every nation under heaven. In short, the vision of early Christianity

---

6 For more on these themes, see my previous work on the subject in *Who We Were Meant to Be*, 77–92.

was that the king was on the throne and was drawing back together the shattered pieces of his royal endowment. To do this, he would commission his people to be his royal priesthood, his ambassadors, and through their labors he would reveal the reality of his reign, step by step and piece by piece, until the full and final consummation of his kingdom.

Christus Victor

Scholars have long recognized that this nexus of ideas—Christ's triumph and reign—affected the way that early Christians thought about their soteriology—that is, their theology of salvation. While all of the familiar themes are present in early Christian texts—salvation as atonement and substitution and the manifestation of God's love to the fullest degree—there was also a pronounced focus on salvation as Christ's victory over enemy powers. By defeating the power of Satan and shattering death's hold on us, Christ has brought us out of bondage and into the liberty of his inheritance for us, as citizens of his kingdom and co-heirs of the promises of his messianic age. This view of salvation is referred to as Christus Victor theology, and it was held as complementary to the traditional themes of atonement, such that together they present a full and beautiful mosaic of the work of Christ on our behalf.

While the Christus Victor theme has long been noted with regard to salvation theology, its influence on the theology of mission has seldom been explored. Yet these very themes—the kingship of Christ and the present reality of his active reign of conquest over the spiritual powers—stand at the center of early Christianity's conception of mission.

In the first evangelistic sermon in the book of Acts, Peter makes the case that Jesus is the long-awaited Messiah. He does so by giving the account of Jesus's death and resurrection, and then says that Jesus has received from the Father the promise of the Holy Spirit and has poured it out upon them. This is a claim that Jesus is the active agent in fulfilling Old Testament prophetic expectations of the messianic age; namely, that through the Messiah, God's spirit would be poured out upon his covenant family. Further, Peter quotes Psalm 110:1 (the Melchizedek psalm) in reference to Jesus—"The LORD said to my Lord, 'Sit at my right hand, until I make your enemies your footstool.'" This is an image of a heavenly enthronement which begins a period of active reign, even of conquest. This verse, says James D. G. Dunn, "runs like a gold thread through much of the New Testament … . Its reference to Christ immediately indicates that in earliest Christian faith Jesus was now to be reckoned … as sharing the one God's rule."[7]

---
[7] Dunn, *Did the First Christians?*, 103.

This quotation from Psalms then leads to Peter's exhortation to the crowd, his call for them to come to faith in Christ. Specifically, his call is for repentance for the forgiveness of sins—a very familiar idea to anyone who has heard a gospel presentation in modern western Christianity. It is important to note the context of that call, however, and to understand it in the way its audience would have. The main message was that the messianic age had begun, attested in the death, resurrection, and ascension of the Messiah, as well as in the fulfillment of some of the promises of that age, not least the prophesied outpouring of the Holy Spirit. Now, because the king is on the throne, the appropriate response is repentance, expressing one's submission to his reign and relinquishing one's position as a rebel. The great benefit now available is the forgiveness of sins, possible in a new way now that the messianic high priest is in the heavenly sanctuary, presenting the once-for-all sacrifice for sins. Repentance was the necessary application of the gospel message, the expected response, but the core of the gospel was all about the kingship of Jesus and the commencement of his messianic reign.

> *The core of the gospel was all about the kingship of Jesus and the commencement of his messianic reign.*

These ideas of kingship and reign are the content which stands behind the core statement of early Christianity: "Jesus is Lord." The title "Lord" carried both theological and political resonances. In the Jewish context, in which "Lord" was the Greek translation of the Hebrew name for God, calling Jesus, "Lord," was a declaration of faith in his divine nature and office. In the Greco-Roman context, where emperors regularly collected titles like "Lord," the Christian message was a startling assertion of Jesus's sovereign kingship.

There is, of course, much more of Jesus's reign yet to come. It is inaugurated but not yet revealed in its full consummation. In the common refrain of contemporary theology, it is "already, but not yet." Thus the response to the gospel call of the kingdom—repentance and forgiveness—becomes a crucial piece of the onward march of Christ's kingdom. When Peter addresses the crowd in the temple in Acts 3, he connects the necessity of repentance to the still-to-come fullness of the messianic age: "that times of refreshing may come from the presence of the Lord" (v. 19). Christ is at the Father's right hand, which calls for the response of repentance, and it is repentance—the turning away from former rebellion and toward glad submission to his reign—which will open the way for the full and final manifestation of that reign. Thus it is the reign of Christ which drives the movement to call people to repentance, and the repentance of the nations that leads toward the consummation of that reign.

One of the great signs of the messianic age was the fulfillment of Old Testament prophecies regarding the nations. Early Christians could point to texts like Isaiah 2:2–3 and claim that their movement's spread around the globe was a clear and definite sign that they were a living fulfillment of the prophet's words:

> It shall come to pass in the latter days
>   that the mountain of the house of the LORD
> shall be established as the highest of the mountains,
>   and shall be lifted up above the hills;
> and all the nations shall flow to it,
>   and many peoples shall come, and say:
> "Come, let us go up to the mountain of the LORD,
>   to the house of the God of Jacob,
> that he may teach us his ways
>   and that we may walk in his paths." (Isa 2:2–3)

The ascension and enthronement of the Messiah had ushered in the great ingathering of the nations, just as the Old Testament predicted. In the words of Isaac of Antioch, "The Lord has sent to the nations ... the mighty scepter from Zion."[8]

A Kingdom and Priests

If the theme of Christ's already-but-not-yet reign is one of the underlying themes of early Christianity's missionary understanding, motivating its onward expansion, there is also a corollary theme worth noting. Early Christians were motivated by their own self-understanding. That is to say, there was a sense that the shape of Christian identity—specifically, the offices which Christians fill within the reign of Christ—defined and motivated their witness to the world. Jesus was both king and priest, and Christians, as members of his mystical body, shared in those identities. They were "a royal priesthood" (1 Pet 2:9), "a kingdom and priests" (Rev 5:10; cf. 1:6), and these were not mere metaphors, but real descriptions of offices to which they were called.

In the ancient world, to call something a "kingdom" or a "reign" usually meant something substantial. "The kingdom of God" was not just a fuzzy way of talking about spiritual truths, nor was the assertion that "Jesus is Lord." A kingdom was a very real thing, an administration with practical outworkings that could be seen and touched. And if it was a kingdom, then it, like all kingdoms, would be administrated through its appointed officers.

---

8 Quoted in Murray, *Symbols of Church and Kingdom*, 48.

To speak of Jesus's reign is to speak of one's own position as an officer of his administration, an ambassador with a job to do. According to Ephesians, we are already seated with Christ in the heavenly places (2:6)—an image that implies participation in his reign. If we are officers of Christ's reign, which is even now being manifested across the world, then part of the duty of the Christian is to represent that reign and facilitate its spread.

The idea of "royal priesthood" speaks to this sensibility. Priests exist to represent the spiritual needs of others, so if we are priests within Christ's reign, that means that we exist for the sake of the non-Christians around us. Rather than viewing those non-Christians as adversaries, acknowledging our own priesthood forces us to see them as our very own people, the ones for whom we minister in the courts of God. They are our parish—the ones for whom we intercede and to whom we proclaim the reality of Christ's beneficent reign. The way we live as royal priests thus becomes an integral part of our mission. Just as personal holiness was a crucial part of biblical priesthood, so our pursuit of holiness is part of our priestly work and our witness to the world. As we will see in the next few chapters, the call to a radically holy form of life was itself a major means of missions in the early church.

> *If we are priests within Christ's reign, that means that we exist for the sake of the non-Christians around us.*

Among the leading ideals of holiness in early Christianity was the development of a wandering monasticism that took Jesus's Galilean ministry as its model. In both the eastern and western spheres of Christian expansion, discrete movements arose in which Jesus's directions for his disciples' mission (as in Luke 10) were taken as a normative pattern for a particular type of religious devotion. Wandering pilgrim-monks sought to live as closely as possible to the manner of life of Jesus and the disciples, to imitate Christ not only in spiritual matters but in lifestyle as well. This all-encompassing attempt at the imitation of Christ did not hold evangelistic ministry as its primary goal, but it was certainly a significant factor therein. As in many other cases in early Christianity, the evidence does not point to intentionally designed programs aimed directly at making converts, but it does point to an immense intentionality toward *living as Christians*, as fully as could possibly be done, and conversions were often the result.

Similarly, Christian expansion often appeared to set its focus more on the establishment of churches (or in some cases, monasteries) than it did on the conversion of unbelievers. Because of its high ecclesiology, holding the value and meaning of the worshiping community as something of earth-shaking importance, early Christian expansion often honed in on the communal aspect of mission over the individual aspect. They were not necessarily focused on "saving souls" (though of course that was an integral part of the picture), but on establishing the worship of God in new communities throughout the whole earth. As historian Peter Brown puts it, "Christians might not convert everybody; but they could, at least, be everywhere."[9] And in raising churches to God in all places, they saw in their own movement the fulfillment of Old Testament prophecies about the messianic age.

It would be fair to say, then, that individual conversions were not always—and perhaps not usually—the primary aim of early Christian missions. The primary goal was simply to be a Christian, in the fullest possible sense, and to establish communities of worship wherever one went. But even if not a primary goal, conversions were, as we will see, most definitely the result.

> *The primary goal was simply to be a Christian, in the fullest possible sense, and to establish communities of worship wherever one went.*

---

9 Brown, *Rise of Western Christendom*, 14.

Chapter 2
Miracles and Martyrdoms
Expansion within the Roman Empire

> **MAJOR FIGURES**
> - Apostles
> - Bishops & other clergy
> - Martyrs
> - Apologists
> - Lay Christians

When we consider the basic facts of the expansion of Christianity within the Roman Empire, the evidence is startling at first. Within the span of three centuries, an obscure cult from the backwater provinces of Palestine became the dominant religion of the empire, counting millions of members. The old polytheistic cult system of Greece and Rome appears (at first glance) to have simply faded away. Many historians have documented the remarkable rise of the Christian religion, describing the *what*, *who*, and *how* of early missions—namely, the means and methods of evangelization, as well as the major characters and events of the story. But the *why* of early church missions has not often been addressed—what was it that motivated Christians to spread the news of their new religion beyond the safe and comfortable boundaries of their own home areas?

This is a difficult question to answer, in large part because our records from that age are fragmentary. There are voluminous Christian writings from the period, but very few that deal with questions of the intentionality of mission and evangelism. The question is also difficult because an assumption lies behind it: that early Christians *ought* to have been motivated, in one fashion or another, for the great task of evangelism. From the standpoint of twenty-first-century Protestant Christianity, the heir of several great mission movements over the past two hundred years, it is easy to assume that early Christians should have been able to see quite clearly what we understand as the plain teaching of Scripture: that it is the task of the church to evangelize and disciple the nations.

Such an assumption, however, might be unfair. Scriptural interpretation has been a fluid discipline over the course of church history, and what is plain to us might not have been plain to them. While Christ's missional purpose is clearly shown in the New Testament—and most clearly in the various

"Great Commission" passages—it is not an exaggeration to say that the New Testament seldom commands missionary activity elsewhere. It would have been easy enough for the early church to assume that the missionary mandate was given to the apostles, and not to every individual Christian. The didactic epistles of the New Testament, including the letters of Paul, missionary par excellence, give little in the way of clear direction for local churches to be active in evangelism. Some passages offer the standard counsels for living a holy life in the view of wider society but leave it at this rather more passive form of outreach.

This caveat is worth noting, because our first glance at early church history can be deceiving. While it's true that the empire was converted to Christianity on a massive scale within a few hundred years, on closer inspection we discover a troubling lack of information about any intentionality in outreach. After the close of the apostolic age, there is almost no evidence of intentional public programs of evangelism.[1] In the late second or early third century, the critic Caecilius described Christians as "a tribe obscure, shunning the light, dumb in public though talkative in the corners" (Minucius Felix, *Octavius* 8.4).

However, an absence of information does not necessarily denote an absence of missionary activity. There was clearly some missionary zeal in the early church, or else the new religion would have quickly petered out. It may simply be the case that we do not possess the right kind of primary sources from which to make an estimation of the early church's missional outreach.[2] Our sources often amount to chance lines in works of apologetics or sermons, along with apocryphal and hagiographical stories written generations after the events they describe. Unfortunately, no one in the patristic era was writing systematic works of missiology. Nevertheless, we can use the sources we do have and gather the bits and pieces which allow us to reconstruct a plausible model of the methods and means by which the Christian faith was disseminated across the Empire. Though there is even less information pointing toward missionary motivation, the means and methods themselves allow us to form some observations on the subject. The ways in which early Christians went about spreading the gospel might give insight into their motivations.

---

1 MacMullen, *Christianizing the Roman Empire*, 33–34; Hinson, *Evangelization of the Roman Empire*, 284.
2 Schnabel, *Early Christian Mission, Volume Two*, 1525–26.

Passive Evangelism

ASPECTS OF EXPANSION
- Innate religious appeal of Christianity:
  Monotheism
  Confidence over death
  Egalitarian social relations
  Morality & virtue
- Charitable deeds
- Martyrdom

In discussing the means of evangelism in the early church, it is helpful to separate the passive from the active means. *Passive evangelism* denotes a lack of intentional activity focused toward the specific goal of converting outsiders. That is, passive means of evangelism would be the regular actions and characteristics of the Christian church which are, in themselves, attractive to outsiders and thus a "hook" that leads to conversion. *Active evangelism*, on the other hand, would include practices intentionally focused on the public display of Christianity and the conversion of outsiders.

While this study is interested in active and intentional means of evangelism, since these more clearly reveal the evangelist's motivations, it should be noted that passive evangelism appears to have been the more vibrant force for Christian expansion throughout most of early Christianity. This form of evangelism was unplanned, not part of a broader program, and it was almost always the fruit of the labors of anonymous lay Christians. As they worked, traveled, and interacted with family, friends, and neighbors, lay believers lived out the principles of their faith in the ordinary details of everyday existence, and in so doing they won many to belief in Christ.[3]

Foremost among the passive means of evangelism was the broad religious appeal of Christianity. It offered a sense of security in being the people of a sovereign God, over against the common cultural fears that one was simply at the whim of fate. Rather than facing the meaninglessness of an existence in which one's life was, at best, a pawn in the hands of capricious pagan gods, in Christianity people found purpose and hope. God's plan for the world was not capricious; it offered an overarching narrative of hope and redemption, clearly revealed in the work of Christ. Further, it was a view of life in which each person could feel that they played a significant part.

The intellectually complex monotheism which Christianity represented was also appealing to many Greek and Roman minds. The inherent irrationality of the traditional depictions of the Greek and Roman pantheons

---
3 See Kreider, *Patient Ferment*, 75.

had disaffected many in the philosophical schools, moving them away from paganism. By the first century AD, many Platonists and Stoics had already come to the conclusion that the universe was created and ruled by a single, all-powerful god, who in broad outline looked something like the God of the Christians (though naturally with some differences in precise doctrine).[4]

Christianity was also remarkable for the way it provided an optimistic hope for life beyond the grave. Death loomed very large in the Greco-Roman psyche, and its presence there was forbidding. The roads into every major city were lined with tombs and monuments to the dead, tombs built to look grand but often striking a note of hopelessness. There was a broad belief that life of some kind continued after death, but it was thought to be a lonely, sad, ghostly life. Roman families took flowers out to tombs (a practice that continues today in many cultures) and held occasional meals there as a way to alleviate the crushing burden of loneliness and despair which the dead were thought to suffer.

In contrast, Christianity told of an afterlife of unimaginable joy. Not only so, Christians believed in the idea of heaven not simply as an abstract doctrine, but as a settled reality confirmed by their present experience of living in a relationship of faith with Christ. Knowing the resurrected one—he who had triumphed over death itself—gave them a confidence over death that was unheard of in the ancient world. Pagan crowds were astonished at the way that Christian martyrs approached their end. Here were people who clearly believed that death had no power over them, and to the Roman mind—in which death was an intractable reality looming over one's life at every moment—this was staggering to see.

> *Knowing the resurrected one gave them a confidence over death that was unheard of in the ancient world.*

There was a confidence in Christian doctrine that was lacking in much of the religion of the empire, and its doctrines were both simple and capable of infinite complexity. Also appealing to some would have been the inclusiveness and egalitarianism of the early church—all people, regardless of age, sex, race, or class, were welcomed and treated as brothers and sisters. This would have been particularly attractive to the poor, to slaves, and to women. There would also have been a strong draw exerted by the sense of universal brotherhood in Christianity—cohesive and united across thousands of miles and countless people, all of whom recognized one another as family.

---

4 See Engberg-Pedersen, "Setting the Scene," 11–12.

Miracles and Martyrdoms

Further, Christianity exhibited a high system of morality, rich with many virtues that would have been appreciated by those grounded in Greco-Roman philosophy, and with a few virtues that went a good deal beyond the old philosophies. The admonition to "love one another" as a basic rule of one's faith, expressed universally toward all people, was a startling novelty to many Greeks and Romans.[5] If there is any counsel toward evangelism in the New Testament epistles, it is generally found on this mark: the tacit appeal of a virtuous life. There seems to be a definite sense that Christians ought to live in holiness because the outside world was watching (for example, see 1 Cor 14:23–25 and 1 Pet 2:12).

This idea of evangelism-by-example took two specific and very compelling forms in the pre-Constantinian church (before 312 AD): charity and martyrdom. It is important not to underestimate the exemplary power of charity, both in generosity and in self-sacrifice. Two separate plagues struck the Roman Empire during the second and third centuries, each with devastating consequences, the first in 165 and the second in 251. In these crises, Christians proved the rule of loving one's neighbor by caring for the sick, even at the risk of their own lives. Concerning such actions, the church historian Eusebius remarked:

> Then, the evidences of the zeal and piety of the Christians became manifest and obvious to all, for they were the only ones in the midst of such distressing circumstances who exhibited sympathy and humanity in their conduct. They continued the whole day, some in the care and burial of the dead, for numberless were they for whom there was none to care; others collecting the multitude of those wasting by the famine throughout the city, distributing bread among all. So it was cried abroad, and men glorified the God of the Christians, constrained as they were by the facts to acknowledge that these were the only really pious and real worshipers of God. (*Ecclesiastical History* 9.8.13–14)

Intimately connected to the impact of charity was the effect of Christian martyrdom on Roman society. In fact, many of those who risked their health to serve the dying considered the act a kind of voluntary martyrdom. Most of the accounts of martyrdom are from Christian writings, and they make much of such events. The perseverance, courage, and unflagging confidence of the martyrs were primarily an inspiration to fellow believers, but there are bits of evidence here and there that such displays of holy zeal made an impact on the pagan audience. *The Martyrdom of Polycarp* (second century) records that the deportment of Polycarp at his execution made such an impression

---

5 Stark, *Rise of Christianity*, 86.

that long afterwards he was "spoken of everywhere, even by pagans" (19.1). Eusebius speaks more strongly yet: "In this the magnanimous confessors of Christ [i.e., martyrs] who shone conspicuously throughout the whole world, everywhere struck the beholders with astonishment and presented the obvious proofs of our Savior's divine interposition in their own persons" (*Ecclesiastical History* 8.13.11). In the face of such death-defying confidence, onlookers would be driven to only two explanations: either the Christians were mad, or there was something unspeakably powerful in their beliefs.

Active Evangelism

> **ASPECTS OF EXPANSION**
> - Lay witness
> - Preaching
> - Ecclesiastical organization
> - Apologetics
> - Exorcisms
> - Temple-smashing

Evidence for active forms of evangelism within the Roman Empire is hard to find. It appears that some clergy were active in public preaching to mixed audiences, but references to such activities are scant. It may be the case that the early church considered its evangelistic ministry to be largely of a passive form—simply to be salt and light by its presence in the world, evidencing the truth of their faith through their day-to-day lives. As Minucius Felix put it, "We do not preach distinctive things; we live them!" (*Octavius* 38.6).

The most common and effective means of evangelism was probably the day-by-day encounters of Christians and non-Christians in the streets, living quarters, and workplaces of the empire's cities—what we might call "personal witnessing." We have little in the way of direct confirmation of this sort of evangelism in the written record, but a few accounts attest to the way that a casual, one-on-one encounter could lead to conversion. Justin Martyr, for example, after a long search through various philosophies to find one that satisfied his questing mind, was finally converted to Christianity through a chance encounter with an elderly Christian whom he found walking on the seashore.

An understanding of the living conditions in Greco-Roman urban centers also leads to the hypothesis that casual, day-by-day contacts were a powerful factor in the evangelization of the empire. As historian Ramsay McMullen notes, "Urban households and groups that were poor, or at least not rich, were obliged to live right on top of each other. Their crowding necessarily exposed them to ideas from their neighbors."[6] While church meetings tended to be secretive after the onset of persecution, it would have been difficult to conceal one's religious adherence in the rhythm of day-to-day living. This was especially so in the case of Christians' non-participation in common public rituals, from frequenting houses of prostitution to making obligatory sacrifices to the gods on civic holidays. Such abstentions would have been noticed. It is quite possible, then, that Christian laypeople served as an effective missionary force simply by modeling a holy lifestyle in the sight of their neighbors, which would naturally have led to conversations about the faith.

The historical record offers us hints of people engaged in intentional works of evangelism, but seldom any direct accounts of their practices. The *Didache* (an early Christian handbook) speaks of itinerant prophets in the Christian community, also attested in other sources, but it is not clear that evangelism was a major part of their work, and some indications suggest that it was not.[7] We have a few hints from the second century of the work done by Polycarp in the area around Smyrna, as well as a reference to a possible practice of Irenaeus preaching in the Lyons area in the local Celtic dialect.[8] The third-century theologian Origen attests to a knowledge of those who "made it their business to go around not only the cities but even the villages and farms that they might win other worshipers to God" (*Contra Celsum* 3.9). Eusebius likewise adds to the story of Pantaenus, who went as a missionary to India, that "there were even there many evangelists of the Word, who were ardently striving to employ their inspired zeal after the apostolic example" (*Ecclesiastical History* 5.10.2).

> *The apostolic and apologetic model made much of the person of Jesus Christ, and particularly of his fulfillment of ancient prophecies.*

Beyond these oblique mentions, however, the topic of evangelistic preaching seldom surfaces in the vast corpus of early Christian texts, and pagan critics of Christianity seldom cite any such activity either. From what evidence exists, however, we can reconstruct some of the basic shape of this preaching. The apostolic and apologetic model made much of the person of Jesus Christ, and particularly of his fulfillment of ancient prophecies.

---

6 MacMullen, *Christianizing the Roman Empire*, 39.

7 See, for instance, the discussion of itinerant prophets in the Pseudo-Clementine literature in Kreider, *Patient Ferment*, 76–77.

8 Latourette, *History of the Expansion of Christianity*, 98; see also Smither, *Mission in the Early Church*, 30–31.

The age of the faith was an important consideration in Christian presentation, so everything possible was done to ground the gospel in the antiquity of Old Testament sources. An ancient pedigree for one's religion was a persuasive factor in Greco-Roman culture, and Christianity was too often mocked as a newly invented religion, offering none of the hoary sanctity of the old myths. But Christians, by pointing to Abraham and Moses as foundations of their religion, and by indicating all the centuries-old prophecy that Jesus fulfilled, could legitimately claim that their faith stretched back into the mists of time even farther than did the legends of Homer or Virgil.

Apologetics was another broad field of evangelistic effort during the early centuries of Christianity. Although apologetic interaction undoubtedly took place in person-to-person contacts, it has come down to us almost entirely in the form of Christian literature. The main goal of the apologists (in whose number are such leading lights as Justin Martyr, Minucius Felix, Tertullian, and Origen) was to defend Christian doctrine and practice against the attacks of its critics. But their aim was more than mere defense. Their essays and treatises were written, at least in part, in the hope of inspiring conversions. Justin Martyr published his *Second Apology* with this very aim in mind.[9] As to their effectiveness, we can say almost nothing. They were evidently widely read and preserved among Christians, but we have little knowledge of their impact on nonbelievers.

> *Often linked with miracles of healing, exorcism was perhaps the most common public presentation of the gospel.*

We have yet to touch on the one public practice of Christianity that is most noted in accounts of Christian/pagan contact, a practice that would surprise some modern Christians: exorcism. Preaching made much of the power of God, either as a patron or an enemy, and it was made clear in those sermons that the power of Christ was far greater than the powers of demons or of fate. This principle was directly displayed in works of exorcism.[10] Often linked with miracles of healing, exorcism was perhaps the most common public presentation of the gospel.

Given the scriptural evidence of exorcism and healing in the ministries of Jesus and the apostles, this trend probably ought not to be surprising. Many pagans regarded the practice with a wary eye, as some sort of trickery, but the influence and fame of Christian exorcists was widespread. Irenaeus, writing toward the end of the second century, claimed that miracles were

---

9 See Green, *Evangelism in the Early Church*, 251–52.
10 Hinson, *Evangelization of the Roman Empire*, 277.

still present in his time, though perhaps tapering off from the frequency they attained in the apostolic age. Origen, about fifty years later, attested to his knowledge of miraculous power still present among Christians.[11] "Exorcist" became an established office within the church (Eusebius mentions it as "an office of special labor"), and by the turn of the sixth century, there were twenty-two exorcists listed as active in Rome.[12]

The sheer ubiquity of miraculous signs in Christian accounts of evangelism leads to the conclusion that it was one of the major engines that drove continued conversion. "Like it or not," says historian Richard Fletcher, "this is what our sources tell us over and over again. Demonstrations of the power of the Christian God meant conversion. Miracles, wonders, exorcisms, temple-torching and shrine-smashing *were in themselves* acts of evangelism."[13] At the very least, the whisperings of such rampant supernatural power in Christianity would have sparked the interest of pagan neighbors.

These practices, such as are listed above, fill out the list of known evangelistic practices of the early church in the pre-Constantinian age. After the conversion of Constantine to Christianity (312 AD), however, other factors emerge. The church had grown significantly in the second and third centuries, but in the fourth, with the approval of the imperial establishment, it exploded. The evangelistic activities already described continued, often in a more public manner than before. Along with these, however, came the dual evangelistic means of social pressure and the use of force. The former is natural and relatively innocuous—as Christianity grew in social stature and wealth, it became more appealing to the upper classes of the empire. Where the prestige is, there the people will soon follow.

More troubling, at least at first glance, is the evidence of the use of force. Once Christianity became the favored religion of the Roman state, immense pressure was leveled against pagan institutions. Leading this charge was Constantine himself—"a man given to bloodthirsty violence"— who, although more moderate in his early years, became an active crusader against heresy and paganism later in his reign.[14] Many of the emperors who followed him took up the same project, seeking the absolute destruction of pagan religion. Historians of late antiquity note a sad litany of violence against pagan temples and their priests, often at the hands of Christians. This violence was most commonly in the form of temple-smashing, although it occasionally included acts of violence against persons as well.

---

11 See Lane Fox, *Pagans and Christians*, 329.
12 MacMullen, *Christianizing the Roman Empire*, 28.
13 Fletcher, *Barbarian Conversion*, 45.
14 Fletcher, 50; cf. Smither, *Mission in the Early Church*, 22.

As Christianity began to deal with the rise of sectarian and heretical groups within itself—Arians, Eutychians, Monophysites, and others—violence could spill over between Christians. This was especially so in Egypt, which, in the words of one historian, "echoed to the shouts of partisans, the din of violence, and laments for those robbed, stripped naked, flogged, imprisoned, exiled, sent to the quarries and coppermines, conscripted into the army, tortured, decapitated, strangled, or stoned or beaten to death."[15]

A word of clarification is necessary, however. Much of the narrative of "Christian violence against pagans" comes not so much from the primary sources, as it does from eighteenth-century reconstructions and expansions of historical themes, many of which—written at the height of Enlightenment fervor—were looking for ways to cast Christianity in a harshly critical light. This Gibbonesque flair for pointing fingers at early Christians is still regularly seen among historians, but there is a growing recognition that the situation was more complicated than the picture such polemics paint.

First, it is important to remember that much of the violence after Constantine's time was expressly political in nature. Once the emperors had hitched their regime to Christianity, then pagan institutions and heretical movements became not merely religious rivals, but a potential source of political instability. Like any ruler in the ancient world, the emperors were keenly set on eliminating rivals, not because of any pietistic motives, but as the natural expression of their political power. Pagans and heretics could be punished as seditious actors standing against the regime, but such violence was rarer than some sources would suggest; the main imperial strategy against paganism was to forbid its outward practices and let it slowly die off on its own. Many of the most famous acts of temple-smashing—like the destruction of the Serapeum in Egypt—were at the behest of imperial orders, and such acts usually took place after the temples had fallen out of regular use.[16]

What about Egypt, though, with its religious riots and roving bands of "monks" who too often functioned as mafia-style thug squads? Egypt's identity as a sectarian-violence hotspot was not due to Christianity in particular; Egypt had been a hotspot of violence for generations. As David Bentley Hart describes Egypt during this period, "At the lowest level of

> **Much of the worst violence comes down not to the fact that some of the rioters were Christians, but that all of them were humans.**

---

15 MacMullen, *Christianizing the Roman Empire*, 93.
16 Hart, *Story of Christianity*, 58–60, 69; see also Berkley, *Formation of Islam*, 33–34; Brown, *Rise of Western Christendom*, 74–75.

society, religion was often little more than a tribal allegiance. Riots were frequent and murderous, and no community was safe from another."[17] In the last analysis, much of the worst violence comes down not to the fact that some of the rioters were Christians, but that all of them were humans, with an innate propensity to see the other as an enemy.

Second, where religious motives were present in episodes of violence, it was generally not a case of using violence to force conversions or in an attempt to eradicate people who held opposing viewpoints. Modern audiences tend to have the image of beleaguered pagans being forced to convert to Christianity at sword-point. That was not the case, at least not until centuries later and in the rarest of instances, and when those rare instances occurred, they were usually roundly condemned by the most influential Christian voices in the empire. John Chrysostom, a church father who served in the highest churches in Antioch and Constantinople, preached that the use of force was always an improper method for gaining conversions.[18] Since Chrysostom's audience included the imperial court, his message was a not-too-thinly veiled warning to the emperor, who was no doubt tempted to use such methods on occasion.

> *The willingness of Christians to enter the grounds of old temples and tear the idols down sent shock waves through communities.*

The most common form of religious violence described in the sources was not against people (especially when one discounts Egypt's predilection for sectarian riots), it was against buildings and statues. Temple-smashing appears regularly in the post-Constantinian era, but usually as a response to specific imperial commands (it was otherwise illegal), and often after the temples in question had been abandoned thanks to imperial restrictions on pagan worship.

Even under those qualifications, however, the act of temple-smashing carried enormous weight, such that it would become a regular missionary tactic in the later advance of Christianity across central Europe. Why was it considered so dramatic and effective? Because it was a demonstrable proof that the power of Christ was greater than that of the old pagan gods. Even if a temple had been long abandoned, people tended to treat it with great respect and trepidation, afraid that any act of contempt against it would anger its god. Local legends regularly included warnings of immediate death by divine power should anyone harm the pagan idol sitting in the temple.

---

17 Hart, 55.
18 Hinson, *Evangelization of the Roman Empire*, 64.

In the context of these beliefs, the willingness of Christians to enter the grounds of old temples and tear the idols down sent shock waves through communities on every side. Not only were these Christians admired for their courage, but when they pulled down the temples without being struck with death or disease, many became convinced of the conquering power of Christ. Conversions were a regular result of temple-smashing, but not because pagans felt cowed by pressure from aggressive Christians. It was because they saw the proof of their old belief's powerlessness right in front of their eyes, and they gladly traded it for allegiance to a greater power. On a few occasions, the pagans most fiercely committed to their faith would spark riots against the Christians in response, but the clear evidence of paganism's paucity of spiritual power was impossible to argue against, and eventually the local impact of pagan cults began to wither away.

As a final statement of Christ's victory over the powers, Christians had a habit of erecting new churches on the foundations of old pagan temples. Nowadays, such an act would fall afoul of critics on both ends of the spectrum. Some might castigate the Christians for cultural appropriation, but in the blended, patchwork religious milieu of the Roman Empire, such a charge is practically meaningless. On the other side, Christians who today eschew anything that might ever have been associated with a pagan background (such as those who object to Christmas trees or to calling Resurrection Sunday "Easter") might find it shocking to see just how readily the early church built its houses of worship on the foundations of old pagan temples.[19]

Both sets of objections fall short, largely because early Christians did not have any interest in appropriating paganism into their religion. Rather, this act represented a religious conviction that God was greater than any other spiritual power in the universe. Christ had defeated the false gods, and therefore they could take over pagan holidays and build churches on pagan ruins as an expression of the absolute victory of Jesus. It was a repudiation of paganism in the strongest possible terms, all based in their conviction that Jesus Christ was the only true king of all creation. The most common motto in Christian artwork from the early centuries was little more than a brief abbreviation, but it underscores the confidence that Christ had defeated all the powers of death, hell, and demonic forces: *IC XC NIKA*, "Jesus Christ conquers."

Agents of Evangelism

One of the overriding features of Christian expansion within the Roman Empire was the activity of clergy. Aside from the possibility of day-to-day, casual contacts by laypeople mentioned above, we have little record of

---

19 See Smither, *Mission in the Early Church*, 115.

Christian laypeople being involved in what we have called "active evangelism" (though, as noted, they were the predominant force in passive evangelism). The historical picture painted for us always has clergy as the major characters in missions. Kenneth Latourette summarizes it well:

> It would probably be a misconception to think of every Christian of the first three hundred years after Christ as aggressively seeking converts. Such pictures as we have of these early communities in the New Testament and in the voluminous writings of these centuries warrant no such conclusion. In none of them does any hint occur that the rank and file of Christians regarded it as even a minor part of their duty to communicate their faith to others.[20]

Most of the accounts of evangelism and mission that have come down to us show mission *through the agency of the church*. Almost every account connects conversion with the founding of a church. This was quite probably the paradigm of early Christian missions—clerics, and bishops in particular, would go out to found a new church through preaching, healings, and exorcisms. More commonly, perhaps, the sequence would begin not with active evangelism on the clergy's part, but by unchurched populations on the margins of Christianized areas contacting a bishop and requesting that someone come and start a church for them. In some areas of the early church, a unique office developed—the *chorepiscopos*—whose function appears to have been that of a wandering rural bishop. Once a church was founded, the passive forms of evangelism, which probably account for the most conversions during the pre-Constantinian period, would take over.[21]

At the forefront of every work of Christian literature from that era are the bishops—writing, preaching, teaching, and binding the church together. Later on, especially in western Europe, monastic institutions took a share in those roles as well. The defining feature, throughout, however, was that evangelism was an action of church offices, and that it was aimed not simply at conversion, but at building new local instantiations of the church.

---

20 Latourette, *History of the Expansion of Christianity*, 117; see also Hinson, *Evangelization of the Roman Empire*, 271–72.
21 Hinson, 33.

The Range of Evangelism

Christianity did not uniformly plant deep roots around the empire. It was numerically very strong in Asia Minor and north Africa; and it had multiple well-established communities in Egypt, Syria, Italy, Greece, and Gaul; but comparatively less so in Palestine, Libya, Spain, and Britain. Those areas with less of a Christian presence also tended to be less densely populated since much of Christianity's early growth happened in cities.

Christianity tended to develop deep roots in the major urban centers of the empire but faced a stiffer challenge in evangelizing the rural hinterland, where up to ninety percent of the empire's population lived. In the eastern provinces, where major urban centers were more common, the surrounding rural areas appear to have benefited from urban Christianization, particularly in Egypt, Syria, and Asia Minor. In the western provinces, however, most of the countryside remained untouched not only by Christianity, but by Romanization as well. Here there lived the local minorities of the empire, regarded as little better than the barbarians that existed beyond the imperial borders.[22] Even in the east, however, the rural countryside could remain largely unreached in some places. In the sixth century John of Ephesus undertook an evangelistic campaign in the rural reaches of western Asia Minor—where Christianity had a major presence since the days of Paul—and found 80,000 people there in need of baptism.[23]

These gaps in the Christian mission effort—rural areas and frontier provinces—may speak to early Christians' understanding of the evangelistic mandate. Later Protestant mission movements would conceive of the missional task in terms of people yet to be reached with the gospel of Jesus Christ, but the historical evidence does not necessarily indicate that early Christians within the Roman Empire shared that view.

Eusebius includes an intriguing story that adds some perspective to this assessment. He records Bishop Dionysius's exile in Libya during the persecutions that were assailing the church in Egypt. Dionysius finds himself among people who "had never before heard [the gospel]," and after reporting that many of these people turned to the faith, he conjectures that it may have been for that very reason that God had led him into exile there. However, he describes his initial reaction as one of emotional affliction. He didn't want to go to "a region destitute of brethren and good men," and he bemoans his condition there, especially his separation from his beloved city.

---

22 Fletcher, *Barbarian Conversion*, 15–16.
23 Fletcher, 62.

While he speaks of the extension of the church in his place of exile, the tone of the story offers us more of a sense of the Christians' love for their own urban communities than any sense of concern for the condition of the unreached (*Ecclesiastical History* 7.11.12–17). He views the conversion of the rural peasantry as a happy side effect of God's providence in protecting him from persecution, but not as a goal worthy of consideration for future programs of intentional outreach.

> *In their eyes, it may not have been so much about the people to be reached as about the theological significance of the mission itself.*

Concern for the conversion of individual unbelievers appears not to have been the primary motivation for mission in the early church. In their eyes, it may not have been so much about the people to be reached as about the theological significance of the mission itself.[24]

Missionary Motivations

For those places and times in which Christians were involved in intentional acts of evangelism and mission, what motivated them to act thus? How would they have articulated their motivation for mission? Several plausible answers can be posited.

Although the textual sources do not offer significant evidence of concern for the spiritual state of unbelievers as a primary motivation, we must remember the old adage that "absence of evidence is not evidence of absence." There are certainly a few texts in which witnessing to one's neighbors was encouraged, even if emotional overtones of compassion might be lacking.[25] Concern for unbelievers may not have been the primary emphasis of early missions, but that does not mean that it was not present at all. Much of the silent expansion of Christianity during the first three centuries must have been a result of casual, day-by-day contacts between believers and unbelievers. If that is true, then concern for unbelievers almost certainly must have been a partial motivation.[26] We need no direct attestations from the early church to form such a claim; it is a logical deduction from the nature of Christianity itself, which commands the love of one's neighbor.

Still, having said that, the juxtaposition of the early church's rather muted texts on the subject of evangelism, and those of later Christians, is striking.

---

24 See Schnabel, *Early Christian Mission, Volume Two*, 1546.
25 Hinson, *Evangelization of the Roman Empire*, 63.
26 Green, *Evangelism in the Early Church*, 249.

Consider the following quote from the nineteenth-century preacher Charles Spurgeon: "If sinners will be damned, at least let them leap to hell over our bodies. And if they will perish, let them perish with our arms about their knees, imploring them to stay. If hell must be filled, at least let it be filled in the teeth of our exertions, and let not one go there unwarned and unprayed for."[27] One searches the writings of early Christians in vain to find such themes expressed in a similar way. Nonetheless, it is impossible to imagine the spread of Christianity without some level of concern for the salvation of one's neighbors, so we must assume that it existed.

Another motivation that we might expect to find is that of obedience to Scripture. However, evidence for any such motivation is practically nonexistent. The Great Commission is seldom referenced, dropping out of Christian writing almost entirely in the second century.[28] Where allusions to the Great Commission are made, they almost always assume that it was a command for the disciples alone, and that the disciples accomplished it, at least in an incipient way. Justin Martyr, in the second century, said of the disciples, "they proclaimed to every race of men that they were sent by Christ to teach the word of God" (*First Apology* 39). Tertullian, writing in the third century, also appears to hold this notion: "His disciples also, spreading over the world, did as their Divine Master commanded them" (*Apology* 21). Similarly, the Christian writer Origen noted, "the voice of the apostles of Jesus has gone forth into all the earth, and their words to the ends of the world" (*Contra Celsum* 1.62). Whether because of their biblical interpretation or because of the limits of their geographical understanding, all of these writers appear to have thought that the worldwide mission commanded by Christ was already accomplished. As such, obedience to biblical commands does not loom large as an early aspect of missionary motivation.

What we do find in the earliest missionaries, however, is the motivating power of gratitude and responsibility. The patron-client relationship defined much of Greco-Roman culture, and it was not uncommon to understand God (or Jesus) as one's divine patron. As such, gratitude was due him, and one way of showing that gratitude was to spread his influence and to magnify his public reputation. If you were the client of a powerful patron in your city, it was expected that you would make it your duty to speak well of your patron, to build him up in the eyes of your friends and neighbors, such that his influence might expand.[29] This cultural lens naturally came to be the way

---

27 Spurgeon, *Spurgeon at His Best*, 67.
28 Green, *Evangelism in the Early Church*, 239.
29 Brown, *World of Late Antiquity*, 37.

that many Roman-era Christians conceived of their relationship with God. If God was your patron, and you were grateful for the benefits of his favor, then you would do your part by magnifying his name to those around you.

By the end of the second century, this sense of grateful obligation came to include the motivations of reward and punishment—namely, building up merit with the divine patron and, at the same time, warding off his punishment. A good client could expect to receive increased attention and favor from the patron, while a poor one might have their requests go unanswered or might even find themselves punished. While such an application of cultural ideas onto one's relationship with God goes beyond the biblical description of the life of faith, it nevertheless appears to have been present in the minds of many early Christians. Justin Martyr reflects this motivation when he gives his reasoning for writing his *First Apology*: "It is our duty, accordingly, to allow everyone an opportunity to inspect our life and teachings, lest, by keeping people ignorant of our ways, we share the penalty due them for mental blindness." A failure to explain the goodness of God to others—that is, to do the work of a good client for one's divine patron—warrants a share in the consequences for unbelief.

Another motivation looms even larger than the patron/client dynamic, and it is a concern to see the reign of Christ manifested in real, this-world, practical ways. Early Christianity, drawing from its Jewish roots, was concerned

> *Early Christianity, was concerned with the supremacy of God in actual experience and not merely in theological abstract.*

with the supremacy of God in actual experience and not merely in theological abstract, and hence with God's triumph over Satan, the demons, and all false religion. The rise of religious violence such as temple-smashing after Constantine's conversion and the official acceptance of Christianity is, as we have seen, a complicated trend to analyze, tied up as it is with political and local/tribal motivations. Nevertheless, the fact that religious violence became such a prominent factor in Christianity's self-expression toward the pagan world indicates that temple-smashing was probably not just a result of new political realities, but that it had roots in the self-understanding of early Christianity.[30]

It has often been noted in theological circles that the early church was dominated by an understanding of the work of Jesus called the Christus Victor model. This model conceives of Christ's work of salvation as a triumph

---

30 Lane Fox, *Pagans and Christians*, 23.

over the forces of sin, death, and Satan. In the strongest form, it conceived of Satan and his demons ruling the world as an occupying, usurping force; every sin was an action which ceded further sovereignty to Satan, as human free will capitulated to Satan's reign to ever greater degrees; and the worship of anything other than the one true God was, in fact, the worship of demons.[31] Into this sorry state of affairs came Jesus, who through his death and resurrection defeated the powers of Satan and reclaimed his own proper sovereignty over all things. Ascended to the Father's right hand, he reigns in glory—a reign that is not merely a spiritual abstraction or a hoped-for future state, but a present reality that can be seen and felt in one's daily life. The vanquished forces of the enemy were still present and still resisting Christ's reign, but the turning-point battle had already been won on the cross, and a full and final victory was assured.[32]

Much of the Christian life, then, was seen through the lens of this theological model. Many believers saw themselves, quite literally, as having been rescued from the kingdom of darkness and brought into the kingdom of light. As historian E. Glenn Hinson puts it, "Converts were enlisted [via the rites and liturgies of the catechumenate and baptism] into the *Militia Christi*, as it were, with an oath which tolerated no other allegiances and were made participants in the battle to defeat Satan and his forces."[33]

Many of the early Christian practices that now seem strange to us find their locus in this theological understanding of the world. Asceticism, for example, the radical practice of total self-renunciation and physical deprivation for the sake of nurturing the spiritual life, was in many ways focused on spiritual warfare. Anchorites and hermits did not steal themselves away into the desert merely for the sake of becoming holy; they went away in order to confront and do battle more directly with demonic forces. Even to put it in those terms obfuscates the truth somewhat, because the goal of becoming holy was itself a form of spiritual warfare: the claiming of the battlefield of one's own heart for the sovereignty of Christ.

So it was with mission. The early church saw in its mission an extension of Jesus's own mission—namely, his continued triumph over the forces of sin and Satan. Evangelism, while necessarily concerned for the individual unbeliever, did not always hold conversion as its primary goal. Rather, mission was driven by the same fierce zeal that drove Phinehas to spear down the Israelite idolater before the presence of the Lord

---

31 MacMullen, *Christianizing the Roman Empire*, 18.
32 See Brown, *Rise of Western Christendom*, 72.
33 Hinson, *Evangelization of the Roman Empire*, 95.

(Num 25:6–13); it was moved by a concern for the glory and honor of the name of God in the world. The nations now belonged to Christ, and so there was every expectation that with Christ reigning from his heavenly throne, the nations would see and submit to his sovereignty. Unbelievers were not primarily viewed as lost souls in need of salvation (though early Christians would not necessarily have disagreed with that portrayal); they were viewed as captives in need of deliverance. Early Christian mission saw itself in the mold of Moses and Aaron confronting the courts of Pharaoh, expecting that the reign of Christ, manifested in their words and deeds, would bring down the oppressive regime of evil spirits which had long held people prisoner.

Seen through the lens of the Christus Victor model, we can now also understand why heresy was viewed not just as a disagreement among fellow Christians, but was sometimes castigated as a demonically inspired error. Everything that detracts from the truth of Scripture and the unity of the church must, in the mind of the early church, derive from Satan, who was vainly trying to forestall the triumphant advance of Christ's kingdom. Some of these heresies, like Arianism, were a significant threat to biblical orthodoxy, but others, like the so-called Nestorianism of the Church of the East or the Monophysitism of the Coptic and east Syrian churches, now look in retrospect like differences in semantics rather than substance. One of the marvelous ironies of early Christian mission is that in many cases, the spread of the gospel was facilitated more by the church's disunity than its unity. The zeal which surrounded its sectarianism, which at first glance appears to have been counterproductive or even cruel, turns out to have translated into effective methods of Christian expansion. As we will see in the upcoming chapters, the competition between various groups of Christians at times ushered in enormous advances in cross-cultural mission.

> Missions were more a matter of the reality of Christ's advancing kingdom, than they were a matter of individual salvation alone.

The Christus Victor model, then, was not just a feature of atonement theology. It was tied to early Christianity's understanding of the mission of the church. In short, that mission was to make real in the world the victory that Christ had already won, and it did this by confronting the powers, preaching the gospel, and showing the goodness, truth, and beauty of Christ's kingdom in daily acts of holiness and love. Even before the conversion of

Constantine, there was a confident optimism in Christian thought which held that Satan was clearly being defeated through the work of the church. This is why exorcisms and healings were among the main means of public evangelism. And this is also why early missionaries were characterized more for their miracles and their shrine-smashing than for their messages of hope to the individual. In short, missions were more a matter of the reality of Christ's advancing kingdom, manifest in the church, than they were a matter of individual salvation alone.

Chapter 3
Empires and Trade Routes
Expansion to the East

MAJOR FIGURES
- Thomas (India)
- Pantaenus (India)
- Addai/Thaddeus (eastern Syria)
- Aggai (Mesopotamia & Persia)
- Gregory the Illuminator (Armenia)
- Nino (Georgia)
- Alopen and other wandering monks (central and eastern Asia)

When we turn to the eastern expansion of Christianity, we are met with a different picture of the missionary impulse than the glimpses we get within the borders of the Roman Empire. Christianity spread early and quickly toward the east, and that region became the heir of a profoundly missional identity that persisted for nearly a thousand years. This chapter will examine the earliest areas of Christian expansion—India, eastern Syria, Mesopotamia, Armenia, Georgia, and Persia—and then follow the later expansion from the efforts of Persian Christians into central and eastern Asia.

While the pattern of expansion differs from that seen within the Roman Empire, many of the same themes reappear. The working of miracles, like healings, arises prominently in some stories. Christian expansion also appears to have been, by and large, expressed through offices and institutions of the church. In some cases, this came in the form of a missionary being sent out in response to an invitation by a foreign delegation; in others, in the form of monastic movements which ordered their lives by a model of ascetic wandering. In each case, the primary emphasis appears to have been the institution of a local, practicing model of kingdom-life in each new area.

India

ASPECTS OF EXPANSION
- Apostolic preaching
- Clerical mission in response to an invitation

There is a long and lasting ancient tradition which says that the apostle Thomas brought Christianity to India in the first century. Though such a missionary journey cannot be definitively proven through the evidence that has come down to us, the tradition is nearly as strong as the widely accepted claim that the apostle Peter met his death in Rome.[1] Two main sources record this early tradition: the first is the *Acts of Thomas*, most probably written in Edessa (east Syria) around the turn of the third century, and the second is the vast record of ancient oral traditions by the churches in India which claim descent from Thomas's work.

The *Acts of Thomas* is a strange book, carrying with it a message of asceticism that is unbiblical in its scope. The main message that Thomas preaches is not quite the gospel as we know it, but rather a gospel that takes its stand against the practice of sexual intercourse. For this reason, the book has been accused of bearing gnostic influences, which it certainly may, but complete sexual renunciation was not unknown in some marginal Christian groups as well, particularly in the east.

Despite its heterodox nature, several intriguing details from the *Acts* have been corroborated by archaeological evidence. The Indian king to whom Thomas was sent is recorded as "Gundaphorus" by name, long considered to be a fictional character. But in the nineteenth century, an amateur British archaeologist discovered clear evidence of a King Gundaphar in the early- to mid-first century, holding sway over a swath of territory from central Afghanistan all the way into the Punjab. A number of other circumstantial data also allow us to consider the possibility of the Thomas tradition. Trade between the Roman Empire and India was well-established during the mid-first century, and in the years before Thomas's journey, Roman ships had discovered the great secret of the monsoon winds, enabling them to set up regular traffic by sea. Indeed, the Edessan author of the *Acts* has Thomas going to India by sea, tracing the very route that first-century merchants were using, down the Red Sea and around the Arabian peninsula. Further, we have independent knowledge of an Indian prince requesting Greek carpenters to build a palace for him in the first century—the very task and role for which King Gundaphar recruited Thomas.[2]

---

1 Moffett, *History of Christianity in Asia*, 30–31.
2 Moffett, 29–32.

Beyond all this, we have the agreement of many early church fathers that Thomas was, indeed, the apostle to India. No rival tradition places him anywhere else (though a few have him making other stops on his way to India). The only question remaining is whether Thomas went to northern India (the Indus/Punjab region), where King Gundaphar lived, or to southern India (the Malabar coast/Kerala), where all the local Indian traditions say he came. Those traditions, eventually written down in the sixteenth and seventeenth centuries, attest to Thomas's missionary efforts on the southwestern coast of India, where he planted seven churches. Both locations for Thomas's work are eminently plausible, and it is not a stretch to imagine that he may have preached in both areas. The local Indian traditions do not hold that Thomas stayed in Kerala; rather, he went off again, preaching his way eastward. Almost every tradition is agreed that he died at Mylapore (on the eastern coast near Madras), where his tomb stands to this day.[3] The dual facts that many early Christian traditions believe that Thomas went to India, and the presence of a lasting Christian community that claims him as their founder, provide compelling evidence for the old story.

In our study of missionary motivations, the next question to ask is, "Why did Thomas go to India?" Few of the local traditions provide a clear answer, but the strange narrative of the *Acts of Thomas* does. In that story, Thomas's motivation is largely one of obedience. According to its account, the disciples had a meeting after Pentecost and divided up the nations by lot, in order to begin fulfilling the Great Commission. (This story, incidentally, was well known in early Christianity, and most of the disciples were believed to have served as cross-cultural missionaries as a result, though none went as far afield as Thomas.) The lot for India fell to Thomas, but he did not want to go. He pleaded with the Lord to be sent anywhere but India. But Jesus appeared in bodily form and made a deal with an Indian emissary of King Gundaphar, selling Thomas as a slave to go and build a palace for the king. Thomas responded with a cry of obedience: "I go wherever you command, Lord Jesus; your will be done!" (*Acts of Thomas* 1).

The next tradition of a missionary going to India comes from the story of Pantaenus, for whom Eusebius and Jerome are our main sources. Pantaenus was the leading teacher of the famous catechetical school in Alexandria near the end of the second century, and he numbered among his pupils both Origen and Clement of Alexandria. According to Jerome's telling of the story, an Indian deputation came to Alexandria and were impressed with Pantaenus, so they asked Bishop Demetrius to send the scholar to India.

---

3 Neill, *History of Christianity in India*, 33–34.

Eusebius doesn't mention this request but says rather that Pantaenus was appointed for the task because he displayed "such ardor and so zealous a disposition for the divine word." Eusebius indicates India as the furthest point of his expedition, but hints that Pantaenus may have had contacts with other "nations of the East." Eusebius also adds a curious detail, namely that Pantaenus discovered a group of Christians somewhere in the east, planted by Bartholomew and possessing a copy of the Gospel of Matthew in Hebrew (*Ecclesiastical History* 5.10). The connection with Bartholomew is often dismissed as an error, but it is not implausible that Pantaenus encountered in the east a group of Christianized Jews of the diaspora.[4]

Eastern Syria and Mesopotamia

ASPECTS OF EXPANSION
- Apostolic preaching
- Miracles
- Wandering pilgrims imitating Christ's mission instructions

The city of Edessa, in the contested kingdom of Osrhoene (now eastern Syria) between Persia and the Roman Empire, quickly became the focal point for the eastern expansion of Christianity. Later traditions, which historians like Eusebius preserve, give a very early date for the Christianization of Edessa. In a rather fanciful tale, Eusebius tells how Agbarus, prince of Edessa, wrote a letter to Jesus during his earthly ministry, to which Jesus responded in a letter of his own (*Ecclesiastical History* 1.13), promising to send a disciple to him. Sometime after Pentecost, the apostle Thomas commissioned Thaddeus, known in the east as Addai, to preach the gospel in Edessa. (According to most early traditions, this Thaddeus was one of the seventy of Luke 10, not the disciple mentioned in the Gospels as part of Jesus's twelve.) Addai went and preached, and with his evangelistic ministry, accompanied by a miraculous healing, the Edessan church was begun.[5]

The account of Addai's mission is historically plausible. As with the story of Thomas to India, early attestations are nearly unanimous that an evangelist named Addai was the father of the Edessan (Osrhoenian) church. What makes the claim more believable is the fact that Edessa, as the mother church for all subsequent eastern expansion, did not follow the common practice of other provinces by claiming one of the twelve apostles as their founder, but

---

[4] Moffett, *History of Christianity in Asia*, 38.
[5] Soro, *Church of the East*, 37–38.

rather a missionary of lesser status.[6] Also, considering the exodus of Jewish Christians from Palestine from the time of Saul's initial persecutions until the fall of Jerusalem, it is not at all surprising that some of those Christians, like Addai, would have gone up to the church at Antioch, and from there followed the trade roads east to Edessa.[7]

The same diaspora probably brought Jewish Christians into Mesopotamia, where various "Nazirite" and "baptizing" sects long persisted, pointing to an early genesis. After Addai's ministry, his disciple Aggai continued the mission, preaching ever eastward into Mesopotamia, and perhaps reaching all the way through Persia and to the borders of India.[8] He was formerly a maker of silk robes (and thus familiar with the trade routes of the east), and it is said in *The Doctrine of Addai* that "instead of gold and silver he enriched the Church of Christ with the souls of believers."[9] While the best traditions have Aggai carrying out his preaching mission in and around Edessa, later traditions name him, as well as two other disciples of Addai, Mari and Pkidha, as the men who brought Christianity into the Assyrian kingdom of Arbela.

Edessa quickly became the theological center of the eastern church. Though later placed under the Patriarchate of Antioch, it was a semi-independent source of theological authority in the east because of its use of Syriac rather than Greek as its liturgical language. (Syriac was a dialect of Aramaic, written in Syrian script, and represented the common linguistic heritage of Mesopotamia and eastern Syria.) The Greek-speaking Christianity of the Roman Empire, partially cut off from the east because of the linguistic divide, did not exert much influence on the formation of Christianity in the east. Edessa, which sat on the trade routes and conversed in both Greek and Syriac, was the bridge. From its theological schools came the ideas that shaped the Persian church, which proved to be one of the most powerful missionary forces in the history of Christianity.[10]

---

6   Moffett, *History of Christianity in Asia*, 50.
7   See Soro, *Church of the East*, 69–77.
8   Baumer, *Church of the East*, 15.
9   Quoted in Moffett, *History of Christianity in Asia*, 49.
10 Moffett, 188–89; Vine, *Nestorian Churches*, 37.

Armenia and Georgia

> **ASPECTS OF EXPANSION**
> - Witness by a captive or slave
> - Miracles
> - Preaching
> - Temple-smashing

Like Edessa, Armenia sat uncomfortably between two very different worlds. It was caught in the power struggle between the Roman Empire and Persia. It was culturally and ethnically associated with the latter, but politics and religion eventually brought it within the fold of Rome. The earliest traditions attribute the first preaching in Armenia to Bartholomew and Addai. In Armenia's case, however, there is little evidence to support either claim. There are traces of early Christianity in Armenia, but not enough to reconstruct a picture of their appearance or growth.[11]

The best and fullest tradition of the Christianization of Armenia grows out of events around the turn of the fourth century. Gregory the Illuminator, the son of an assassin who had killed the king of Armenia, returned to that country after growing up in exile in the Roman Empire, where he had become a Christian. Upon his return, he was promptly imprisoned by King Tiridates (Drtad), the now-grown son of the murdered king. Some years later, however, a disease befell Tiridates. The writer Agathangelos, in his hagiographical recounting of the story, has it that Tiridates was transformed—either physically or mentally—into a boar, much as in the biblical story of Nebuchadnezzar. Gregory was brought from the prison, and after preaching to Tiridates and the royal court for sixty-five days, the king was healed. Tiridates, along with a great multitude of his people, became Christians.

Some of the details of the story are likely an embellishment, but the historical figures of Gregory the Illuminator and King Tiridates remain constant in the tradition. All of this took place before Emperor Constantine's Edict of Toleration, thus making Armenia the first officially Christian nation in the world. (A rival claim is held by the Kingdom of Osrhoene, of which Edessa is the capital, said to have become Christian by 200 AD, but as it was no longer an independent kingdom a century later, the claim loses some of its force.[12]) According to Agathangelos's story, King Tiridates joined with Gregory in his ministry, going throughout the length and breadth of the land to preach and to remove pagan temples.[13]

---

11 Arpee, *History of Armenian Christianity*, 9.
12 Jenkins, *Lost History of Christianity*, 54.
13 Arpee, *History of Armenian Christianity*, 17.

A rather similar story emerges of the evangelization of nearby Georgia, another ancient principality of the Caucasus. Here the protagonist is Nino, a young woman who witnessed to the royal house of Georgia in the 320s AD. Like Gregory the Illuminator, she had grown up in the Christian faith within the Roman Empire before her arrival in Georgia. Sources differ on how she came there—one of the main traditions (Rufinus's *Church History*) has her as a slave, brought to Georgia in captivity, but another says that she had fled there to escape persecution in Armenia. In any case, her testimony of faith won the royal household to Christianity after they began experiencing miracles of healing. The queen, one of Nino's first converts, was healed from a long and chronic illness. King Mirian III, who initially resisted the new faith, was healed from a bout of blindness when in desperation he decided to pray to the God of Nino. Shortly after his conversion, the king declared Christianity the state religion of Georgia.

Persia & Central Asia

ASPECTS OF EXPANSION

- Wandering pilgrims imitating Christ's mission instructions
- Monastic practices
- Clerical & lay missions
- Ecclesiastical organization

Sources are insufficient to reconstruct a full picture of Christianity's initial spread in Persia. Aside from Aggai and his associates, it is difficult to identify any individual missionaries highlighted in the tradition. What emerges is not an individual portrayal, but a communal one: mission as the result of monastic expansion. Early Egyptian monasticism was characterized by an eremitical life of personal seclusion in the desert, but early Syrian monasticism was of a more mobile variety. Monks were wanderers, going about among the towns and villages, preaching the gospel and exemplifying a holy life.[14] These monastics, known in the east as the Sons and Daughters of the Covenant, were at times so numerous that they appear to have constituted a large part of the church.[15] However, because the ascetic monastic ideal—especially the virtue of celibacy—was so prominent in their practice, the native Persian populace never fully embraced that form of Christianity.[16]

---

14 Moffett, *History of Christianity in Asia*, 77–78.
15 Moffett, 98–99.
16 Waterfield, *Christians in Persia*, 30–32; see also Baumer, *Church of the East*, 78.

Parthia (the name of the Persian Empire under its Arsacid rulers) was a religiously tolerant place, and Christianity had freedom to propagate the faith. That situation changed quickly, though, when in the year 226 a new dynasty came to power—the Sassanids, who were fiercely committed to Zoroastrianism, the ancient faith of Persia. Under certain rulers of the Sassanid empire, Christians were subjected to longer and fiercer persecutions than any undergone by Roman Christians, and yet, surprisingly, the Persian church suffered far fewer apostasies than its Roman sister.[17] Perhaps as a result of this violent persecution, it never won more than a small minority of the Persian people. Constantine's association of Christianity with Roman power was a further blow to the spread of the gospel in the east, because Rome was indisputably the enemy, and thus Christianity was regarded with a wary eye. Most of the persecutions undergone during the Sassanid dynasty were motivated as much by politics as by religion.

The fifth century brought theological separation between the east and the churches of the Roman Empire. An ecumenical council rebuked the teachings of Nestorius and declared them heretical. Followers of Nestorius, who largely resided in Syria, fled to the east. The Persian church at first had no particular stake in the theological controversy. However, because of their connections with the theological schools of Edessa, they had a deep and abiding affection for the work of Theodore of Mopsuestia, the great biblical commentator who also happened to be one of Nestorius's teachers. In the east, he was regarded as the definitive voice in biblical interpretation, and when the council denounced his works as heretical, a schism began. The Persian church, though it came to be known as Nestorian, was quite probably not heretical, and the schism was a result more of a disagreement over Theodore of Mopsuestia than over any of Nestorius's teachings.[18] In common convention, the ancient Mesopotamian/Persian church does not refer to itself as Nestorian (though the title has traditionally been applied to them); it takes the name "the Church of the East."[19] Both terms will be used interchangeably here.

> *The fifth century brought theological separation between the east and the churches of the Roman Empire.*

It was after this theological break that the Nestorian church came into its full flower of missionary activity. Because Nestorianism had been condemned

---

17 Waterfield, 145; see also Jenkins, *Lost History of Christianity*, 57.
18 Waterfield, 171–73, 200–201.
19 Baumer, *Church of the East*, 7–8.

by imperial Christianity, the Persian political aversion to it was now somewhat muted.[20] By the sixth century, according to the writings of Cosmas Indicopleustes, there were Nestorian Christians in Socotra, southwest and central India, and possibly as far as Sri Lanka, Burma, and even Vietnam. Such advances often came via the agency of monks—east Syrian hermits had developed several traditions of how to live an ascetic life, and one of them was to wander about and emulate the manner of Jesus's life. As Christoph Baumer says of them, "Hermits were prepared to place their seemingly inexhaustible inner strength in the service of missionary work, to which the rapid expansion of the Church of the East to the east and south attests."[21] We have records of Nestorian Christians engaging a mission to India and finding the native Indian heirs of the Thomas churches. These Indian churches were strengthened by an influx of Nestorians fleeing occasional persecutions in Persia.

Nestorian Christians pressed even further east, following the Old Silk Road all the way into central China, where they were welcomed in 635 by the ruler of the T'ang dynasty.[22] Alopen, the Nestorian monk who led the mission, won the favor of the emperor, T'ai Sung, and earned the right to spread Christianity within his realm.[23] There they built churches and monasteries and remained as a religious presence for at least the next 300 years.[24] The Nestorians' most impressive missionary efforts, however, were to the north and east, bringing the gospel to the Turkic tribes of Bactria and central Asia, even as far as Mongolia, and in some cases translating Scripture into local languages as well.[25]

It is no exaggeration to say that the expansion of the (Nestorian) Church of the East represents one of the greatest missional movements in the history of Christianity, far surpassing the geographical extent of Roman Christianity at the time. The eastern church pressed on relentlessly, crossing national, cultural, and linguistic boundaries, and ultimately planting churches across a vast swath of the largest continent—an achievement within that region that is still largely unrivaled to this day.

These missionary efforts contain certain distinctions that are worthy of note, especially in contrast to the early missions in the Roman Empire. Many of them seemed to be intentional. It was not merely a process of religious

---

20 Vine, *Nestorian Churches*, 42–43.
21 Baumer, *Church of the East*, 128.
22 Waterfield, *Christians in Persia*, 43–44.
23 Smither, *Mission in the Early Church*, 42.
24 See Moffett, *History of Christianity in Asia*, 302–14.
25 Jenkins, *Lost History of Christianity*, 63.

osmosis or incidental contacts. Nestorian missionaries were sent out with the express purpose of planting churches in new areas. There also arises from the records a significant sense that the missionaries had a definite concern and love for the people to whom they went. Most strikingly, these missions included not only clergymen, as in the Roman Empire, but laymen as well. The structure of this missional expansion nevertheless resulted—as in the Roman west—in the establishment of new bishoprics in communion with their mother churches. Mission, although taking a somewhat different method, was still focused not only on gaining converts, but on producing new local instantiations of Christ's church.

Missionary Motivations

What motivations lay behind the vast geographical spread of the eastern church? If missions within the Roman Empire were motivated by a theology of Christus Victor, the same can be said of the east, especially in the case of the wandering monks. The Sons and Daughters of the Covenant were initiated into the Christian faith as if into an army, and they were pledged to destroy the works of Satan. The motives behind their work were expressly tied to a Christus Victor view of the world.

But why the model of wandering monasticism rather than of seclusion, as was prevalent elsewhere? The answer is probably both cultural and theological. In the east, with a heavier influence from Jewish-Christian roots than was present in some of the western churches, theology developed more in the direction of practical applications than abstract doctrine. The churches of Syria and the east were suffused with a functional and incarnational theology, much as what is found in the book of James. The eastern tradition was characterized less by theological disputes and more by its care of the poor. Further, with roots going back to Thaddeus/Addai of the Seventy, the pattern of wandering evangelism as demonstrated in Luke 10 would have been one of the foundations of their tradition.

Another explanation of the eastern church's success has to do with the view of the world engendered by one's geographical placement. Within the Roman Empire, Christians were a part of an independent, self-standing political and geographical system—connected with other areas, to be sure, but in such a way that they were sure they were at the center. Very few ventured beyond the borders of the empire, where they saw only barbarians or enemies. It was a consciously self-contained world.

The east, by contrast, was far more open. Its trade routes had forged connections with distant provinces for millennia. The surrounding territories were not the realms of uncivilized anarchy, but of profoundly ancient and well-ordered societies. Living in the Persian Empire, Christians were well aware of the great civilizations of China and India to the east, which they regarded as neither enemies nor barbarians. Expansion in the east faced less of an obstacle based in social prejudice than it did in the west.

Eastern Christianity would have also been conscious of the outward movement of their religion from the Mediterranean basin to their own territory. Christianity was a faith in motion, and thus it would seem natural that it keep moving. Since a missional movement had brought Christianity to them, mission became interwoven in the fabric of the faith they received. The east Syrian father Aphrahat, reflecting this sensibility, referred to the Christian community as "the Church of the Nations."[26] Eastern Christianity saw itself as a movement that was both global and perpetually active. This highlights one of the clear features of early Christianity's most significant mission movements: they were built on self-perpetuating cultures of missional identity, a theme that will be explored in more detail in chapter 9.

---

26 See Murray, *Symbols of Church and Kingdom*, 57.

Chapter 4

The Call of the Desert
Expansion to the South

> **MAJOR FIGURES**
> - Desert monks (Arabia)
> - Frumentius (Abyssinia)
> - Julian & Longinus (Nubia)
> - Donatists (Berber North Africa)

We now turn to examine the spread of Christianity in those geographic areas to the southeast and south of the Roman Empire—namely, Arabia and Africa. Precise evidence as to the means and motivation of evangelism is somewhat harder to come by here, since only a few ancient authors devote any space to the affairs of those regions.

The exception is the case of north Africa (which, for the purposes of this study, consists of the southwest Mediterranean coastal strip of western Libya, Tunisia, and Algeria, and which in the Roman Empire encompassed the provinces of Africa, Numidia, and Mauretania). Although north Africa was properly understood as part of the empire, and much of the content of chapter 2 applies to the north African context in the first three centuries, we are dealing with it in this chapter to examine the spread of Christianity after Constantine's conversion. North Africa had both a mixed population and a position along the Saharan frontiers, so it is worthwhile to inquire about its missionary activity in the period after its cities had already become Christian. In the writings of the early church, the region receives a great deal of attention in areas of doctrine and church practice; unfortunately, the authors that speak of it—even its own residents—seem to have little to say about missionary efforts.

We will examine four regions in turn: in the case of Arabia, Ethiopia, and Nubia, we will seek to answer the question of missionary motivations. For north Africa, however, our study will focus on the reverse: why there seems to have been a lack of missionary zeal there, despite having one of the most deeply rooted Christian presences in the empire.

Arabia

> **ASPECTS OF EXPANSION**
> - Political affiliations
> - Monasticism
> - Sectarian rivalries

It is best to begin with a description of the boundaries used to designate Arabia, because they vary somewhat from the modern conception. "Arabia" as a Roman province designated the Transjordan area also known as Nabatea, and it was there that Arabian Christianity began in New Testament times. Paul said that he sojourned in Arabia, and doubtless he witnessed to the gospel there. For our purposes, we include not only the province of Nabatea, but all areas during the first five centuries AD where Arab-related people groups lived. Most of these groups spoke a form of early Arabic; others, especially in the north, used Aramaic. Geographically, this area includes the eastern part of modern Syria, western Iraq, all of Jordan, Saudi Arabia and some of the other nations of the Arabian peninsula, and parts of southern Israel and the Sinai.

Lying directly beside of the birthplace of Christianity, it was natural for Arabia to benefit from the religion's growth. The borders of the Roman Empire were more tenuous and fluid than modern borders, and trade routes and cultural connections made for a close fellowship between the Arabian interior and the Roman provinces of Palestine, Nabatea, and Syria. Most of the spread of Christianity into that region could be described as a form of osmosis. Rather than being the result of intentional missionary efforts, this early spread of Christianity was probably driven by the simple, day-to-day meetings of Christians with Arabs. As would be expected, then, Christianity in Arabia found its deepest roots in those areas that lay near regions with older Christian communities—Palestine, Mesopotamia, and Ethiopia.[1]

But other than the untraceable impact of merchants, travelers, and incidental contacts, what were the primary means of evangelism in Arabia? First and foremost was a passive means—the power-appeal of the Roman Empire. By the time that Arab communities began to turn en masse towards Christianity, it had become the religion of the empire. To be Christian was to gain the friendship of the empire and to make an important ally. The gravity of this imperial sphere of influence was enough to cause the mass conversion of some Arab monarchs and their tribes in the fourth and fifth centuries.[2]

---
1 Latourette, *History of the Expansion of Christianity*, 233.
2 Smither, *Mission in the Early Church*, 14; Latourette, 234.

The opposite, however, was also true. There were groups of Arabs who did not want to be absorbed into the Roman/Byzantine sphere, and so they sought a path that would set them apart as distinct. Heretical Christian sects thus made deep inroads in Arabia, because they offered a clear means of keeping one's own people independent from the orthodox power of Constantinople.

Another means of evangelism was the presence of miracles. The chronicler Sozomen tells of an Arab sheikh in the late fourth century who was converted, together with his whole tribe, because he was promised a son if he became a Christian. He consented, and soon after the promised son was born, he and all his tribe were baptized.[3] Similarly, we hear of a sheikh's paralytic son being healed by a monk, and his whole tribe coming to faith as a result.[4]

In almost all of these accounts, the agents of healing were monks. Monasticism, particularly of an eremitic variety (that is, solitary hermits), became the first deep exposure of many Arab nomads to Christianity. Two of the more prominent early monks to penetrate Arabia were Hilarion and Moses. Hilarion was the founder of a monastic movement that occupied much of the Negev desert, and Moses is reputed to have converted a whole tribe and later (if indeed it is one Moses, and not two) to have been appointed bishop to a group of nomads.[5] Though these monks evidently did not go out with the express purpose of converting Arabs, their method of spirituality brought the two groups into contact. These anchoritic monks retired to the desert to live as hermits, and it was in the desert where the nomadic Arabs lived. This austere desert spirituality appealed to Arab sensibilities in a way that the intellectualized urban Christianity of the empire never could. Where we do find accounts of evangelism, it is almost always desert monks who are the missionaries.

> *Where we do find accounts of evangelism, it is almost always desert monks who are the missionaries.*

Perhaps the most unique feature of Arabian Christianity, and one that ties in with its expansion, is the issue of heresy. Heretical interpretations were so often associated with Arabia that it developed into a catchphrase: *Arabia haeresium ferax* ("Arabia fertile in heresies," itself a pun on an earlier popular description, *Arabia felix*—"happy Arabia").[6] Some of the tendency

---

3 Trimingham, *Christianity among the Arabs*, 95.
4 Latourette, *History of the Expansion of Christianity*, 233.
5 Trimingham, *Christianity among the Arabs*, 105–7.
6 Trimingham, 56.

toward heresy came from the close affiliation of Arabian churches with the east-Syriac tradition that found its early voice in Edessa. These were certainly regions fertile in speculative interpretations. Edessa tended to be a stopping point for heretical groups that were pushed eastward out of the empire. Mesopotamia had its share of early aberrations, including some odd Jewish-Christian sects. And Marcionism, the second-century heresy which was refuted fairly quickly by the apologists within the empire, persisted in Syria and the eastern marches well into the fifth century.[7]

Arabia itself was associated with the error of Beryllus, and subsequently, along with much of the eastern Church, it kept a deep affection for Origen even after his views were declared to be outside the bounds of orthodoxy. One of the most missional sects was that of Julian of Halicarnassus—Afthartodoceticism—a late development from Egypt in the sixth century. Eutropius, one of the devotees of this sect, ordained and sent off ten bishops throughout Arabia to spread their message. They were somewhat successful, and the sect spread south to Ethiopia and took root there.[8]

It was in the fifth century that the position that defined many of the eastern and southern churches came to take root in Arabia: Monophysitism. This was one of the dissenting views from the decision of the Council of Chalcedon, but it was widespread across the east, and especially in Syria, Palestine, and Egypt. As the Chalcedon-approving government in Constantinople began bringing its power to bear on the doctrinal issue, many Monophysite bishops and monks were faced with either conversion or exile. Historian J. S. Trimingham describes the result:

> The monks were given the alternatives of conformity ... or being turned out into the desert. The majority chose the desert, and as a result, wandering as they did, frequently in groups, among the peasant population and semi-nomads, they consolidated among them their beliefs, which means the people's acceptance of their celebrations of the cult and rejection of priests who followed the established church.[9]

Similarly, the Arab communities around the Persian Gulf probably benefited from the presence of exiled Christians who fled from the Sassanid persecutions in Persia during the fourth century.[10] Thus, persecution and exile brought heterodox forms of Christianity deep into Arabian territory and proved one of the major vehicles of Christian expansion there.

---

7 Trimingham, 53–54.
8 Vantini, *Christianity in the Sudan*, 49.
9 Trimingham, *Christianity among the Arabs*, 164.
10 Latourette, *History of the Expansion of Christianity*, 234.

Christianity in Arabia did not long survive the rise of Islam. The most probable reason is that for Arabs, Christianity had never ceased to be a foreign religion. Christianity's deepest roots were in areas aligned with major power centers—orthodox Byzantium, Monophysite Egypt, Nestorian Persia, and Ethiopia—rather than in the nomad-Arab heartland of the peninsula. Further, the Christianity they knew was splintered and sectarian.[11] While the sectarianism of early Christianity had in some ways driven the expansion of the faith, in other ways it laid the foundations of movements that stepped even further beyond the bounds of biblical orthodoxy. Islam, in the view of early Christianity, was just one more movement in that mold.

The Christians of the seventh century did not appear to treat Islam's rise as the appearance of a new religion. They tended to regard it as the rise of yet another Christological heresy.[12] That is, they saw it as a deeply flawed Christian interpretation, which compiled many of the earlier errors of Arians and Ebionites into a new form. It was clearly too far afield in its theology for any established churches to have communion with it, so it spread unchecked by any significant Christian attempt to rein in its new doctrines. In an Arab milieu in which Arabia had been consigned to an independent whirlpool of heretical sects, believers in the new Islamic faith had no reason to feel beholden to the religious authority of Constantinople, Rome, Edessa, or Alexandria.

Early Christians thus underestimated Islam, assuming that it would likely not amount to a religious threat greater than any previous heresies. There were also other reasons why Islam was able to flourish even in areas which had seen a Christian presence for centuries. Perhaps the most significant oversights were cultural and linguistic. Christians tended not to translate their liturgy or Scriptures into Arabic, and so Arabian Christianity never truly developed a firm Arab base.[13]

Ethiopia

Aspects of Expansion
- Witness by chance encounter
- Clerical mission by invitation
- Sectarian rivalries

The story of Christianity's arrival in Ethiopia in the fourth century is an interesting one. Two men, Frumentius and Aedesius, wards of the Tyrean

---
11 Berkley, *Formation of Islam*, 24.
12 Donner, *Muhammad and the Believers*, 223; Smither, *Mission in the Early Church*, 88–89.
13 Moffett, *History of Christianity in Asia*, 281.

philosopher Meropius, were stranded in Ethiopia when their master died in a pirate attack and shipwreck there. The two men were taken into Ethiopian society and later rose to positions of power. They became the tutors of the crown prince, Aeizanes, who upon his accession to the throne made Christianity the state religion. Frumentius traveled to Egypt to consult with the great church father Athanasius and to request a bishop for the people of Ethiopia. Athanasius responded by ordaining Frumentius to that very post, and thus Ethiopian Christianity had its official beginning.[14]

In the fifth century, Syrian missionaries arrived, remembered in Ethiopic lore as the Nine Saints, and carried out a ministry of planting monasteries and translating the Bible into the Ge'ez language. Given the events of that time, it is probable that these Syrian missionaries were Monophysite exiles.[15] From those early movements of Christianity, the Ethiopian church flourished in relative isolation, taking its lead not from Constantinople or Rome, but from the Monophysite church of Alexandria. Its influence spread northward to Yemen and westward into Nubia.[16]

Here again we see two of the major means of evangelism that also occurred in Arabia—monasticism, brought by the Syrian missionaries; and the influence of sectarian theology (in this case, Monophysitism). But we also see a further means from the story of Frumentius, one that repeats itself in many fringe regions during the fourth through the sixth centuries—emissaries from such regions going into the empire to request a missionary presence. As with Frumentius and his request of a bishop for Ethiopia, many groups took the initiative to contact the emperor or church authorities and ask for a Christianizing presence among them.

Nubia

> **ASPECTS OF EXPANSION**
> - Political affiliations
> - Clerical mission by invitation
> - Sectarian rivalries

The story of Nubian Christianity rests on only a few witnesses, but those few witnesses left a gripping and detailed account. It is worthy of note that Christianity's advent in Nubia (southern Egypt/northern Sudan), primarily in the mid-sixth century, is remarkably late considering the early depth of Christianity in Egypt, immediately to the north. This is perhaps a reflection

---

14 Meyendorff, *Imperial Unity and Christian Divisions*, 118.
15 Isichei, *History of Christianity in Africa*, 32–33.
16 Vantini, *Christianity in the Sudan*, 49.

of a general lack of missionary impulse toward those beyond the imperial borders. Despite the contacts between Nubia and Egypt via the Nile and the concourse of desert hermits with their neighbors, Christianity seems to have made few inroads into the southern kingdoms. Acts records that an official of Candace (which is the Meroitic title of a Nubian/Kushite queen), a eunuch, was converted and baptized by Philip, but if he spread Christianity in his homeland, no record of it now remains. Rather, the first major evangelistic effort toward the Nubian kingdoms of Nobatia, Makuria, and Alwa came in the sixth century, driven by competition between the Chalcedonian and Monophysite sects.

This post-Chalcedon rupture of the eastern Christian world was intense and, ultimately, permanent. Imperial power usually (but not always) supported the Chalcedonian position, which came to be regarded as orthodox, and exerted its power to limit dissenting views. Nestorianism was expelled beyond the eastern marches of the empire. Monophysitism was also pushed back, but it remained dominant in some important areas, and nowhere more so than in Egypt. The Egyptian position on Monophysite Christology was held with such passion that the Egyptian bishops at the Council of Chalcedon thought their lives would be in peril if they agreed with the Council's formulation.[17] It was in the midst of this volatile dynamic that we find the early forays of Christianity into the kingdoms of Nubia.

> *It was in the midst of this volatile dynamic that we find the early forays of Christianity into the kingdoms of Nubia.*

As was the case with Frumentius in Ethiopia, the story begins with the Nubians taking the initiative to request a missionary presence, likely with political benefits in mind.[18] Egyptian historian John of Nikou tells us that the king of Nobatia (the northernmost Nubian kingdom) asked Emperor Justinian to send missionaries into his country. Justinian agreed, apparently for the political benefits of expanding his orthodox sway into the regions of the Upper Nile, especially since neighboring Egypt was so radically Monophysite. Justinian's delegation, which followed the Chalcedonian creed, set off for Nobatia. Meanwhile, the Monophysite faction, hearing of this development, appealed to Empress Theodora, herself a Monophysite sympathizer. Behind her husband's back, Theodora sent a missionary named Julian to Nobatia and gave instructions to the governor of Egypt that everything possible should be done to ensure that Julian reached the

---

17 Isichei, *History of Christianity in Africa*, 29.
18 Welsby, *Medieval Kingdoms of Nubia*, 31.

Nobatians before the Chalcedonian delegation arrived. In this, she was successful. The Nobatians accepted Monophysite Christianity from Julian and rejected Justinian's Chalcedonian missionaries.[19]

The story does not end there, though. Based on archaeological discoveries, it seems that a Nubian kingdom further up the Nile, Makuria, accepted the Chalcedonian form of Christianity, and looked to Constantinople, rather than to the Monophysite church in Alexandria, for leadership. It is possible that Justinian's missionary delegation, having been rebuffed by the Nobatians, carried the gospel further on and introduced Chalcedonian Christianity to the Makurians; or that the Makurians simply wanted a different sect to adhere to for political reasons, setting them apart from the neighboring Nobatians.[20]

This conflict between Chalcedonians and Monophysites had one more drama to stage in Nubia. Some time after the missionary Julian's death, a Monophysite named Longinus began to grow concerned about the state and progress of Christianity among the Nobatians. So he journeyed south and lived with them for six years, building on the introductory work of Julian and setting up the Nubian church in an official form.[21] Just as Longinus was leaving Nobatia, messengers were sent out from Alwa, a Nubian kingdom even further up the Nile, beyond Makuria. They had heard of Longinus and his ministry, and they wanted him to come to Alwa, to evangelize and baptize them into the Christian faith. But this time it was the Chalcedonian party that caught wind of the development and set out to waylay it. Two Chalcedonian bishops were sent to Alwa to plant the faith there and to explain the truth about Longinus's heterodox ways, but the king of Alwa would have none of it. He turned back the Chalcedonian bishops, saying that he wanted no one but Longinus who had ministered among the Nobatians. Eventually Longinus was able to make his way to Alwa after a long, dramatic flight through the desert to circumvent the traps set for him by the Chalcedonian Makurians. Thus the people of Alwa converted to the Monophysite form of Christianity.[22]

In Nubia, we see a familiar pattern: native peoples beyond the imperial borders contacting Roman authorities and requesting a missionary presence, coupled with the influence of post-Chalcedon sectarianism. There are hints in these stories, however, that some of the missionaries had a definite concern and affection for the Nubian people, a sentiment that is not always present in the records of early imperial missionary activity.

---

19 Vantini, *Christianity in the Sudan*, 37–39.
20 Vantini, 89.
21 Welsby, *Medieval Kingdoms of Nubia*, 35.
22 Vantini, *Christianity in the Sudan*, 44–47.

North Africa

> **ASPECTS OF EXPANSION**
> - Ecclesiastical organization
> - Sectarian rivalries

When we consider the Christian churches of north Africa (modern Algeria, Tunisia, and western Libya), we come up against an entirely different scenario, and one that has puzzled many historians. For the first four-plus centuries of the church, up to the ministry of Augustine of Hippo, north Africa had one of the most densely populated Christian presences in the entire empire. According to historian Stephen Mitchell, "The African churches made up by far the strongest and most numerous Christian communities in the western Roman Empire."[23] Bishoprics multiplied there at an astonishing rate, and the north African church produced many of the greatest luminaries of the early centuries: Tertullian, Cyprian, and, of course, Augustine himself. However, after the time of Augustine, the church in that region suffered a long decline. Eventually, some two hundred years after the great church father had taken his rest, Christianity in north Africa buckled and almost completely disappeared in the face of the Muslim invasions.

How was it that the most vibrant Christian provinces could fall so far? A number of answers present themselves, but foremost seems to be the class structure of that area. Three distinct classes appear in the historical record: the wealthy, urban Latin speakers; the Punic-speaking middle class, descended from the Phoenician colonists of ancient Carthage, whose role was that of working the land and other small business ventures; and the native Berber peoples, a semi-nomadic assortment of clans who lived in the rural hinterlands and the desert. In general, Christianity had its deepest roots among the Latin speakers, along with some exposure to the Punic population and apparently little penetration into Berber society, except possibly in the case of the Donatist heresy.[24]

Despite its Latin-heavy center of gravity, we know that Christianity made some inroads into the Punic elements of society, because Augustine made it a requirement that the bishop of the see of Fussala would be able to speak Punic.[25] There is also some evidence that the Donatist faction of Christianity had contacts with Berber society, and Augustine's mother Monica appears to

---

23 Mitchell, *History of the Later Roman Empire*, 280.
24 Latourette, *History of the Expansion of Christianity*, 91–93.
25 Holme, *Extinction of the Christian Churches*, 19; see also Smither, *Mission in the Early Church*, 45–46.

bear a Berber name, so it is not unreasonable to say that Christianity must have had some influence on that segment of the population.

Even with these exceptions taken into consideration, however, the generalization holds true: the north African church was profoundly weakened by the fact that it was never fully accepted as the religion of the Punic and Berber populations. Another weakening factor was the structure of the church itself. Priests and holy men so separated themselves from society in their drive for righteousness that they often provoked ridicule rather than admiration.[26] Further, while Christianity in Syria and Egypt was preserved in part by the strength of the monastic movements there, north Africa had no comparably deep system of monasticism in place to serve as a shield against the religious monopoly of Islam.[27]

North African Christianity was also weakened by its tendency for schism. Worthy of particular note is Donatism. It held that the church must be characterized by absolute purity and that priests and believers who had fallen away during persecutions should be allowed no recourse to return to the faith. Though it was only marginally influential elsewhere in the empire, Donatism was a vast and powerful force in North Africa, rivaling the influence of orthodox groups.

During the time of Augustine, yet another schismatic view was introduced into north Africa. In the early fifth century, the invading Germanic Vandals swept down through western Europe, crossing the Strait of Gibraltar into north Africa. They seized Carthage and set up a kingdom there, all the while acting as patrons to their preferred version of the Christian faith—Arianism—and subjecting other Christian groups to severe persecution. In the end, orthodox Christianity prevailed over both Donatism and Arianism, but it was a hollow victory in north Africa. When the Muslims arrived, they found a Christianity that was deeply wounded by these old fractures, and within a few generations of the beginning of Muslim rule, only a few Christians remained.

> *The main failure of north African Christianity was its inability to overcome the barriers that divided classes in its society.*

At its heart, though, the main failure of north African Christianity was its inability to overcome the barriers that divided classes in its society, or to send out missionaries along the trade routes into the Sahara (which Muslims later did, to great effect). The Christianity of north Africa was rooted in

---

26 Holme, 30.

27 Isichei, *History of Christianity in Africa*, 44.

the towns and was largely limited to the Latin tongue. When the terrors of the fifth century struck—the Vandal invasion, followed by harsh famines, plagues, and the encroaching effects of desertification—many of the Latin Africans fled north to Italy. Thus the collapse of north African Christianity was not so much a result of the conversion of Christian populations to Islam as it was the wholesale transplanting of the Christian upper class.

Why was it that Christians in north Africa seemed to be so little concerned with the tasks of mission and evangelism? In the words of one historian, "One of the mysteries of church history lies in the way in which some Christian communities but not others feel a strong commitment to evangelization. Despite a gloomy view of the eternal fate of the unbaptized, Augustine and his compatriots seem to have felt no duty to preach Christianity beyond the Roman boundaries."[28] It is not the case that they were unaware of the presence of people groups who as yet had no access to the gospel. In one of his theological debates, Augustine argued against Hesychius that "there are among us, that is in Africa, innumerable barbarian tribes among whom the gospel has not yet been preached … yet it cannot rightly be said that the promise of God does not concern them" (cf. Prosper of Aquitaine, *The Call of All Nations* 2.17).[29] Yet as historian Richard Fletcher notes, "Augustine did not follow the logic of the argument to its conclusions: therefore we must send out missionary preachers."[30]

This is a puzzle that affords no easy answer. However, if early Christians held a conception of mission centered on the triumph of Christ and the establishment of his reign, rather than by a primary concern for the individual souls of those who had not yet heard the gospel, then it might be easy for such Christians to slip into a blithe assumption that the main work had already been done. Living as they did in a society where the religion of Christ had already triumphed over the formerly pagan worship of their home cities, evangelism might seem like a low priority. Further, there was a significant amount of prejudice in the Roman Empire against those who lived beyond imperial borders. They were viewed as barbarians (a term we inherit from that very historical context), and so the class-stratified features of north African Christianity might have played against the likelihood of upper-class Latin Christians considering the plight of "barbarian" groups.

North African Christianity, while so strong in tradition, piety, and doctrine, largely failed to undertake evangelism across cultural or linguistic boundaries. Whereas the church spread to Arabia, Ethiopia, and Nubia

---
28 Isichei, 41.
29 Quoted in Fletcher, *Barbarian Conversion*, 31–32.
30 Fletcher, 31–32.

through the fortunate accident of circumstances, the influence of monasticism, and by invitation from other people groups, none of these factors seems to have played a significant role in the Christianization of north Africa. The Christianity that was shown to the Punic and Berber peoples was apparently unsatisfying, perhaps because of its cultural and linguistic exclusivity, and perhaps because of its sectarian dimensions. In any case, north African Christianity, despite its depth in some areas, proved to be shallow in its outreach, and as a result, it has left no living tradition in that area to witness to its ancient vibrancy.

Missionary Motivations

The areas south and southeast of the Roman Empire offer a puzzle to anyone seeking to understand missionary motivations. In this region, the story of Christian expansion smacks of the haphazard and the inconsistent. The spread of the gospel often seems attributable to sheer chance (like Frumentius's shipwreck) or to less-than-sincere motives (like the political maneuverings in the evangelization of Nubia). In some cases, this region feels like it presents lessons in what not to do, rather than practical insights for missionary endeavors.

Nevertheless, this region does provide some valuable food for thought. As a case study, it underscores the negative argument made in this book: namely, that early Christianity did not articulate its motivation for missions in the same way that many current Christians do. Some of the motivations we might expect to find—concern for the spiritual state of unbelievers and a sense of obedience to biblical commands—are even harder to come by in this region than in other areas of the study.

Beyond that broad assessment, two main features of the story stand out from this region. First, it shows once again the place of monasticism in the story of early Christian expansion, exemplified in the spread of the gospel on the Arabian borders and in the Syrian mission to Ethiopia. Monastic models of the Christian life, formed around the radical pursuit of holiness, continued to draw interest and attention to the message of Jesus.

Second, the importance of doing mission within the ecclesiastical structure of the church is again underscored. The evangelization of Nubia was undertaken by ecclesiastical delegates responding to an invitation, and their first acts included the establishment of churches. One of the main features of Frumentius's mission to Ethiopia was to seek the support of the church of Alexandria. Outreach to lower classes in north Africa, where it occurred, appeared to be grounded in the weekly worship and preaching of local churches, whether orthodox or Donatist. In all these cases, mission was a direct extension of the life of the church. The worshiping community took a central role in launching each missional outreach and in constituting the main goal of that outreach.

Chapter 5

Barbarian Gospel
Expansion in Central Europe

MAJOR FIGURES
- Ulfilas (the Goths)
- Martin of Tours (Gaul)
- Clovis & Clotilde (the Franks)
- Columbanus (western Europe)

Greco-Roman civilization did not look kindly on its neighbors to the north. Central and eastern Europe, especially in the regions beyond the Danube and the Rhine, were the home of a vast array of ever-moving people groups, warlike bands who spoke early dialects of the German language family. To the Greek and Roman ear, however, the words they spoke sounded like nonsense. The stereotyped image was of someone just rambling through repeated syllables: "Bar, bar, bar, bar." As such, the imperial world called them "barbarians"—nonsense speakers. Even after the Roman Empire weakened and the Germanic tribes began to make alliances with the emperor, acting as his federated allies in the borderlands, the people of the empire did not raise their opinion of the barbarians. Nor did they see the newcomers as worthy of imperial identity, even when the barbarians admired, emulated, and adopted Roman culture and manners of life.

In addition to the Germanic tribes, there were also the remnants of the empire's longstanding rural inhabitants, many of whom (especially in western Europe) were of ancient Celtic stock. They, too, like the German newcomers, were often regarded as barbarians, usually designated by the pejorative term "rustics." There remained a gulf between the two groups—Romans on one side, and Germans and Celts on the other—a gulf marked by the perception that the virtues of civilization were the inheritance of Rome alone. As such, the spread of the gospel among Celtic and Germanic-speaking people was often a slow affair, and when it did proceed quickly, it was through the agency of Celtic and Germanic missionaries.

The Goths

> **ASPECTS OF EXPANSION**
> - Witness by a naturalized captive
> - Bible translation
> - Political affiliation
> - Sectarian rivalries

The great frontier of cross-cultural missions in the Mediterranean world, from the reign of Constantine to the turn of the second millennium, was to the north, across the vast scope of central and eastern Europe. The people groups who inhabited these territories can be conveniently understood as composing three large groups, two of which have already been mentioned: the Celts, who were by far the foremost inhabitants of western and central Europe during the early Roman Empire (but which, by the time of Christian evangelization, had come to be relegated to certain pockets in the west, namely Ireland, Wales, and the rural areas of Gaul); the Germans, who conquered much of the western empire in the fourth and fifth centuries; and the Slavs, who came to inhabit eastern Europe and the Balkans during the middle period of Byzantine power.

When Christianity began to expand north beyond the borders of the empire, it was the hour of German ascendancy, and the Goths were the most powerful of the German confederations. There were several different tribes of Goths, including the Visigoths and Ostrogoths, who came from eastern Europe and the Balkans to sweep down into Italy and take control of the western empire. Also closely related were the Vandals, who proceeded from central Europe through Spain and into north Africa during the time of Augustine of Hippo, and the Huns, who made a brief but violent incursion nearly all the way to Rome in the mid-fifth century.

Our best and earliest sources that speak of the conversion of the Goths focus on the Visigoths (and more specifically, two groups of Visigoths known as the Tervingi and Greuthungi), who at the time were inhabiting the territory just north of the Danube, where it empties into the Black Sea. The first hints of the dawn of Christianity among the Visigoths come from accounts of bottom-up evangelism—namely, prisoners of war taken from Christian regions who then shared the gospel with their captors. One example of this is Eutychus, a Cappadocian (from modern Turkey) who was taken violently by the Goths and there, in their own country, he spread the seeds of the faith (see Basil of Caesarea, *Letter* 164).

There is evidence of a strong influence from Cappadocian Christianity on Gothia, from the end of the third century through the beginning of the fifth.[1] Basil, one of the so-called Cappadocian Fathers, seems to have had a strong affection for Gothic Christians. There is also a record of a certain Theophilus, bishop of Gothia, who attended the Council of Nicea in 325, where the Arian heresy was condemned.[2] (Arianism claimed that the Son of God was a creation of God the Father, and that therefore he had not always existed with the Father.)

From these first contacts with Christianity, there seems to have grown a small, indigenous movement of Visigothic Christianity. It is this indigenous faith that eventually produced the great missionary figure of Gothic-Roman interactions, Bishop Ulfilas (sometimes rendered Ulfila or Wulfilas). Although the accounts of his life are somewhat contradictory, since both orthodox and Arian historians claim him as their own, most reconstructions have Ulfilas coming to faith under the orthodox tradition, having been born into a captured Greek family of Cappadocian descent, but then later becoming Arian.

As a young man Ulfilas went to Constantinople, probably as part of a Gothic delegation on the event of Emperor Constantine's death, and there he was recruited by the imperial court. Though it was now the post-Nicene era, the heresy of Arianism was still powerful, and Constantius II, the emperor, and Eusebius of Nicomedia, one of the most powerful churchmen in Constantinople, were both sympathetic to Arianism. Ulfilas became a partisan of their version of the faith, and so it was as an Arian or semi-Arian that he returned to his homeland to preach the gospel. Since this was the same area in which he had come to the faith, it is possible that some of his converts were converts from Cappadocian-influenced orthodoxy (rather than from paganism).[3]

However, Christianity was still a minority faith among the Goths, and Ulfilas's success against Gothic pagan religion prompted a backlash persecution. According to church historians, Athanaric (one of the Visigothic rulers) repressed the new faith because the ancient tribal religion was losing power. In response to this persecution, Ulfilas led his flock out of Gothia and sought asylum in imperial territory, where he spent the remainder of his life near the city of Nicopolis. Ulfilas is most remembered not for his preaching or his missionary leadership, but for his translation work. He invented the Gothic alphabet and translated the Bible into Gothic (with the exception

---

1 Sivan, "Ulfilas's Own Conversion," 378.
2 Mathisen, "Barbarian Bishops and the Churches," 670.
3 Sivan, "Ulfilas's Own Conversion," 381–83.

of the books of Kings, which he thought would give unnecessary martial encouragement to the already-too-warlike Goths). In this, he represents perhaps the first translator of the Bible into a previously unwritten language, and his translation stands as one of the earliest in church history.

What can we discern of the missionary motivations of those who went to the Goths? Unfortunately, we know next to nothing of the original Christian contacts. The most probable means of early conversion was the bottom-up method from the influence of captive Christians. As such, they were not intentionally pursuing missionary service, but they may well have engaged in it once they were in Gothia. Ulfilas was not a missionary in the conventional sense of the word. He went to an already Christianized community within Gothia, the people to whom he had already been naturalized. In this respect, he is not greatly different from Frumentius in Ethiopia. The majority of Ulfilas's flock may not have been of Gothic descent, but naturalized Christian expatriates living in Gothia. From the records that survive about the Ulfilian community, we find no great evangelistic impulse among them.

However, although Ulfilas is by far the largest character to emerge from this clash of peoples and religions, he stood only at the beginning of the Gothic movement to Christianity. The great change was to come some thirty years after his exodus. The Huns, a warlike, nomadic people from central Asia, were moving steadily westward, and in 375 they collided with the Greuthungi Visigoths along the northern shore of the Black Sea. The Greuthungi king fell in battle, and his followers fled into Tervingi territory. This began a chain reaction which destroyed the balance in the region and left the Goths feeling insecure about their position. A large contingent of the Tervingi, led by Fritigern, sought asylum across the Danube in imperial territory. Some church historians see this event as the immediate cause of the Goths' conversion to Arian Christianity. The emperor at the time was Valens, a semi-Arian, and it appears that a pledge on the part of Fritigern to accept Arian Christianity was a part of the negotiations that allowed the Tervingi to cross the Danube.[4] The historian Sozomen, in delineating the reasons why the Goths had become Arians (as opposed to adherents of orthodoxy), brought it down to two main causes: Fritigern's pledge to Emperor Valens in 376, and the ministry of Ulfilas.[5]

> *The most probable means of early conversion was the bottom-up method from the influence of captive Christians.*

---

4 Heather, "Crossing of the Danube," 292–93.
5 Heather and Matthews, eds., *Goths in the Fourth Century*, 106–7.

Those two events represent the clearest direct evidence we have for the conversion of the Goths. But it was certainly not the end of the story. Somehow, following this mass conversion of one group of Tervingi Visigoths, all of the major branches of the Gothic people adopted Arian Christianity. Interestingly, though, none of this growth appears to be a result of imperial missionary activity. The Goths moved quickly into the western empire, and in the west there was no practice of consecrating bishops for barbarian peoples, as there was in the east (usually upon request).[6] There remains no historical record for several centuries of any official missionary undertaking by clergy toward the "barbarians" of central Europe.[7] On the contrary, it appears that it was Visigothic missionaries who went out to their fellow Germanic tribes, as recorded by the historian Jordanes:

> Moreover, from the love they [the Visigoths] bore them [other Germans], they preached the Gospel both to the Ostrogoths, and to their kinsmen the Gepidae, teaching them to reverence this heresy, and they invited all people of their speech everywhere to attach themselves to the sect.[8]

But why would Arianism be so fully embraced? The kinship of Germanic peoples can offer some explanation, but, as we saw above, the earliest roots of Gothic Christianity were primarily orthodox. A few other explanations fill out the picture. The conversion of Fritigern and his people in 376 did not mark the end of Gothic-Roman hostilities. In 378 the conflict flared up again, and Emperor Valens marched out to meet the Visigoths in battle, only to be squarely defeated at Adrianople. This landmark victory brought great prestige to the Goths, and they would have taken it as a sign of divine favor for the Visigothic Arian faith (regardless of the fact that Emperor Valens was of the same faith, since Nicene orthodoxy was the official imperial position on Christian doctrine).

Further, almost all of these early Germanic tribes converted to Christianity only after they were within the borders of the empire, conquering and settling across Italy, Gaul, and Spain. Only the Rugi accepted Christianity while still living in the barbarian hinterland. This may be evidence that the choice to convert was a deliberate response to the civilization that confronted them. These Goths were converted with dueling inclinations—first, that of admiration for the depth and beauty of Roman civilization and religion (evidenced by the fact that early Gothic rulers in the western empire modeled themselves after classical Roman emperors); and second, the desire

---

6 Mathisen, "Barbarian Bishops and the Churches," 667.
7 Cusack, *Rise of Christianity in Northern Europe*, 48.
8 Quoted in Cusack, 46–47.

to remain distinct and preserve their tribal heritage. Into this tension came the Visigothic Arian missionaries, offering a brand of Christianity that was different from imperial orthodoxy. So the choice for Arianism may well have been a deliberate choice—to become Christian, as the empire was, but not under the authority of the imperial brand of Christianity.[9]

Whatever the cause, Arianism was embraced not only nominally, but passionately by the Goths. A traveling, warlike people, they consecrated their own bishops to accompany their armies in the manner of military chaplains.[10] The Arian Vandals were so firm in their beliefs that they immediately began persecuting local Catholics and Donatist Christians upon their arrival in north Africa. Even the Catholic historians of the time note the enthusiastic nature of Gothic Arian faith.[11] Not until the start of the sixth century, long after Arianism had been put to rest among Greeks and Latins, did the tide begin to turn back toward Catholic orthodoxy among the Germanic peoples of Europe.

In considering this stage of Gothic history, what else can be said about missionary motivation? All we have is the account of Jordanes and his fellow historians, who tell us that the Visigothic missionaries were motivated by a sense of love for their fellow Germans. This is important to note, because, as we have seen, it was rare that love for the people being evangelized was the primary motivating factor for missions in the early centuries of Christianity. In this case, however, it was a love extended to those perceived as one's own kind, rather than love for those beyond the borders of one's own cultural identity.

Rural Gaul

> **ASPECTS OF EXPANSION**
> - Miracles
> - Temple-smashing
> - Ecclesiastical organization

We now turn from the eastern side of the empire to the west—namely, the province of Gaul (modern France), which had long been under imperial rule. It is considered here, rather than in the section devoted to mission within the Roman Empire, because it ceased to be under Roman control during the period in question.

---

9   Cusack, 46.
10 Mathisen, "Barbarian Bishops and the Churches," 680.
11 Cusack, *Rise of Christianity in Northern Europe*, 49.

Although Christianity came to Gaul no later than the mid-second century (and probably as early as the mid-to-late first century), it did not make significant inroads into the rural countryside. After more than two centuries under Roman rule and Christian influence, the countryside was still the domain of the old Celtic peoples, who worshiped their ancient gods in sacred groves.[12] It was only toward the end of the fourth century, at the same time as the conversion of Fritigern's Visigoths, that this situation began to be addressed through such men as Martin of Tours.

Martin was bishop of Tours from 371 until his death in 397. We know more about that region, the Touraine, than any other part of Gaul in this period, largely because of Martin's biographer, Sulpicius Severus, and the later work of Gregory of Tours. So it is possible that there were other itinerant evangelists in Martin's mold during that time, but if so we simply do not know as much about them.

Martin stands out as unique in the historical record. Rather than living in his bishop-house in the cathedral town of Tours, he lived with a group of monks and traveled about the countryside, converting the locals through demonstrations of spiritual power. It is important to emphasize his monastic connection, because while most accounts focus on his episcopal office, he probably thought of his own identity more in monastic terms, having been deeply influenced by the monasticism of the east.[13]

Perhaps the best way to understand Martin, though, is through the image of a soldier. He was converted while serving in the Roman army, and when he appealed for a discharge, he said, "Hitherto I have served you as a soldier; allow me to become a soldier of God …[for] I am the soldier of Christ" (Sulpicius Severus, *The Life of Martin* IV). Later, as a churchman, he retained that self-understanding. He saw himself as a soldier engaged in God's battle against the powers of Satan, and his methods of evangelism were downright confrontational. He performed miracles of healing, actively disrupted pagan rites, and razed pagan temples to the ground.

It was dangerous work because of the resistance he faced, so his imitators were few and far between. In the year 397, three clerics who were trying to follow Martin's methods by disrupting a pagan rite were all killed by the worshipers.[14] The "rustics," as they were known, were not easily convinced that they should give up their old gods, who had so often provided fertility and good crops. In Martin of Braga's words, they couldn't see why they could not "worship God and the Devil at once."[15]

---

12 Stancliffe, "From Town to Country," 43.
13 Herrin, *Formation of Christendom*, 69.
14 Fletcher, *Barbarian Conversion*, 44.
15 Quoted in Hillgarth, ed., *Christianity and Paganism, 350–750*, 54.

Despite these challenges, Martin was not alone in his ambition to bring the rural countryside to Christianity. Several clergymen in Gaul have left us letters and sermons addressing wealthy landowners, exhorting them to build churches on their properties for their rustic farmers to worship Christ rather than demons. On the other hand, the vast majority of Christian writings and official church documents are silent on the matter of the pagan rural population. This evidence parallels that of Christianity within the Roman Empire for the first few centuries: There was very little in the way of organized, intentional effort toward evangelism or missions, and those few examples of active evangelism seem to be primarily motivated by displays of power against opposing spiritual forces.

We do not know how successful the ministry of Martin was, because within a hundred years of his death, the situation in Gaul—even in the countryside—changed dramatically. During this period the rural Celtic population largely disappeared from the record of history, replaced by the invading Germanic tribes from the east. Although the Vandals and Visigoths both marched through Gaul and inhabited it for a time, the Germanic tribe that became the dominant power there was the Franks (from which modern France derives its name). The Franks appear to have been pagans upon their entry into the empire, but the Arianism of their Germanic cousins was already exerting some influence.

The Franks

Aspects of Expansion

- Political affiliation
- Sectarian rivalries
- Clerical mission by invitation
- Monastic practices
- Wandering pilgrims imitating Christ's mission instructions

The Franks, like many of the earlier Germanic invaders, ended up claiming their territory on the inside of the existing Christian civilization. In a pattern often repeated during the decline of the western empire, the invading Germans admired the depth and beauty of Roman-Christian society and tried to imitate some of its cultural trappings. Upon entering Gaul, the Franks encountered churchmen and lay Christians wherever they went. Further, in what was one of the most important developments in their conversion, they began to take Christian wives from the local population.[16]

---

16 Cusack, *Rise of Christianity in Northern Europe*, 76.

The classic case study in the conversion of the Franks is that of Clovis (Chlodovech in the vernacular; the later French name Louis is derived from Clovis). He became king of the Salian Franks in 481 and was one of the early rulers of what would come to be known as the Merovingian dynasty.[17] He is notable in history not merely for his conversion to Christianity, but because he was the first Germanic king to accept orthodox Christianity, thus signaling the beginning of the end for German Arianism.

In Clovis's case, the primary evangelist was his wife, Clotilde, a Burgundian princess and an orthodox Christian. The turning point for Clovis came in a battle against the Alamans. Finding the tide turning against him, Clovis prayed in desperation to Jesus. According to legend, he promised to be baptized if Christ would give him the victory. And miraculously, the battle turned and Clovis triumphed over the Alamans.

Even after this, however, Clovis was cautious. His wife Clotilde called Bishop Remigius of Rheims to come and instruct him, but he feared that his war chieftains would not take kindly to his change of faith.[18] In early German society, the power of the king lay in the support of the leading warriors, his *comitatus*. Devotion to the pagan gods was a key part of Germanic warfare. If Clovis could no longer lead them to victory in battle, then the warriors would withdraw their support. According to the *Chronicle of St. Denis*, Clovis made an appeal to his chieftains in a general assembly, hoping to convert them to the faith (1.18–19, 23). His people were willing, deciding to follow "the God whom Remigius preaches," and the Frankish king was baptized, together with his entire army of 3000 men.[19]

From this story we find four elements which characterize the history of the conversion of the north-Germanic peoples: (1) the story revolves around the conversion of kings, (2) the influence of Christian queens, (3) the power of Christ to give victory in battle, and (4) the caution with which the king accepts the faith, and only after affirmation by his chieftains. In the case of Clovis, it is also worth noting that active attempts at organized Christian evangelism from Christian clergy did not happen until requested by the queen.

Bishop Avitus sent King Clovis a letter in 496, exhorting him to "offer a part of the treasure of Faith which fills your heart to the peoples living beyond you, who, still living in natural ignorance, have not been corrupted by the seeds of perverse doctrines [i.e., Arianism]."[20] Rather than sending out his own missionaries, the bishop assumed that the German Franks would be

---

17 Fletcher, *Barbarian Conversion*, 102–3.
18 Fletcher, 103–4.
19 Brown, *Rise of Western Christendom*, 89.
20 Quoted in Hillgarth, 78.

in a better position to evangelize their fellow Germans. This hope did not play out in the way Avitus may have envisioned. Clovis was indeed an agent of the spread of Christianity, but it came in the way of political advances against his Arian German neighbors rather than through missions to the unreached.[21]

The Merovingian kings were Christians from the baptism of Clovis onward, and they gained significant control over ecclesiastical appointments in Gaul. The pattern quickly emerged that clerical offices were given in reward to service to the crown, a system which did not serve to add spiritual depth to the Frankish church. The chieftains and ordinary folk were nominally Christians, but there is no evidence that their devotion went any deeper than a patriotic attachment to their Christian king. As historian Eleanor Duckett notes, "In this Christian Frankland of the sixth century pagans were still busy in their ritual, witches in their craft, ignorant peasants in their worship of nature and of the mysterious spirits which they believed to haunt tree and lake and spring."[22] It was not until a hundred years later, toward the end of the sixth century, that the picture again began to change.

In 590 Columbanus, a missionary from Ireland, began his ministry in Gaul, which in time would revolutionize the Frankish church. (His name is sometimes rendered Columban, but in either case it is important to differentiate him from another prominent Celtic missionary, Columba, of whom more will be said in the next chapter.) Columbanus was not a missionary in the modern sense of the word. His primary goal was not necessarily conversion, but rather to build communities in which the monastic life was possible. He was among the classic pilgrim-saints of the Celtic church, and he decided to use the latter part of his life to go wandering among the Franks. His methods were far from the normal course of religious practice in Gaul (and thus he incurred the wrath of both the local clergy and the Frankish royalty), but in time they produced a revival of lay devotion.

> *His primary goal was not necessarily conversion, but rather to build communities in which the monastic life was possible.*

Columbanus went first to Burgundy, where he, along with his twelve Irish monks, founded the monastery of Luxeuil. Curious seekers of the monastic life joined their company, and soon two more monasteries were founded. Columbanus enforced a rigid rule of discipline. It was partly due to his influence that the observance of penance moved from being a

---

21 Cusack, *Rise of Christianity in Northern Europe*, 79.
22 Duckett, *Wandering Saints*, 120.

public, once-in-a-lifetime event in response to a significant moral failure to a frequent individual discipline.[23] He quickly came to be seen as an enemy of the Burgundian royalty, mostly due to his denunciation of a sinful royal union, and he was forced to move on.

During this stage of his life, having already embraced a lifestyle of wandering amid unfamiliar and hostile cultures, Columbanus embraced the call of mission to non-Christians. In a letter written in 610, he made a vow "to make my way to the heathen to preach the gospel to them." He even had it in mind to preach the good news to the as-yet-unreached Slavs to the east, but apparently was warned away from this ambition by Christ in a vision.[24]

He wandered with his fellow monk, Gall, through the kingdoms of eastern Gaul before finally settling in Lombardy, where he founded the monastery of Bobbio. At each place he stopped, he preached to the local pagans. He and his associates managed to spread the gospel among the Alamans, Varasci, Basques, Flemish, and Suevi peoples.[25] This activity stood in contrast to their contemporaries, the Frankish clergy:

> It was here that the Merovingian church failed so dismally. One searches through the sixth-century synods in vain for demands that priests should teach the people about Christianity … . There is surprisingly little interest shown in the Christianization of the countryside, and the few rulings that are made consist mostly of prohibitions.[26]

This legacy of Columbanus, of planting self-reproducing monasteries which would preach the gospel to the surrounding areas, eventually made a great impact on the regions of Gaul, northern Italy, and southern Germany. Columbanus's brand of missional monasticism succeeded not because of his personality, but because it met the religious and social needs of the Frankish society of the time. His new way of doing penance was seized upon enthusiastically by the Franks, who, being portrayed in most contemporary accounts as a murderous, treacherous people, apparently felt the need of regular confession. This change of custom allowed for a heightened growth in lay devotion.

Further, Columbanus's brand of monasticism was rural, as opposed to the urban and suburban monasticism of the Latin west. The Franks were a traditionally rural people, so there was an immediate appeal. These new monasteries also gave the rising Frankish aristocracy the opportunity to act as sponsors through financial gifts and land endowments, and thus to express

---

23 Fletcher, *Barbarian Conversion*, 138–39.
24 Fletcher, 142.
25 Cusack, *Rise of Christianity in Northern Europe*, 79.
26 Stancliffe, "From Town to Country," 59.

their devotion in a way that underscored their status.[27] Because of these developments, Columbanus and his monks were able to provide ways for the Franks to express and grow into their own practice of Christian devotion.

Missionary Motivations

The expansion of Christianity into central Europe is not one of the resounding successes in the history of missions, at least not in its early stages. As in many places within the empire, the rural countryside remained relatively untouched by Christian influence for several centuries. Martin of Tours is a standout figure partly because he is so exceptional; most bishops were not interested in doing the sort of rural outreach in which he engaged. In those places beyond imperial borders, the agents of evangelism were not usually cross-cultural missionaries in the early period, but sectarian groups bearing the message to their own kinsmen: Arian Goths evangelizing other Goths.

In the case of the Goths, compassion for others is directly attested as one of their motivations for spreading the word about Jesus. However, it is clear from the texts that this compassion was rooted in their sense of cultural and linguistic relation. Christian Goths cared for the spiritual state of other Goths because they were Goths. If we look for a sense of concern that crosses cultural and linguistic boundaries, it is harder to discern. With the possible exception of Martin of Tours and a few others, Roman Christians show little evidence in the sources of being concerned for the spiritual welfare of barbarians.

In Martin's case, while concern for the rustics was no doubt one of his driving motivations, it does not appear to have been his main one. He emerges as a prime example of Christus Victor theology as a missionary principle. His goal appears to have been not just individual conversions, but the wholesale deliverance of tribes and villages from the oppressive spiritual regime of false gods. By destroying sacred pagan monuments, he was demonstrating the greater power of Christ so that those who had been held captive to falsehood could go free.

The conversion of the Franks under Clovis follows a common narrative in Christianity's expansion in Europe, often repeated in later generations: a king comes to faith after a miracle or a significant victory in battle, thus making Christianity the official faith for his kingdom. While such conversions ought not to be assumed as insincere, they clearly also carry with them the weight of political calculations. The conversion of the Franks in this manner allowed orthodox Christianity to establish a significant foothold in the Germanic

---

27 Fletcher, *Barbarian Conversion*, 139–140.

world, but it also set a precedent for the political conversion of whole nations, which would later come to be abused under leaders like Charlemagne, leading to the forced national conversions of conquered peoples.

With Columbanus, however, the story takes a different turn. Columbanus represents a branch of the Celtic mission movement, of which more will be said in the following chapter. He is a representative of a new kind of missional monasticism, driven by the pursuit of an ideal Christian life. While much of Columbanus's journey can be viewed as a quest to find a place where he could live a life of quiet prayer, there does also seem to be genuine concern for people who have yet to hear the gospel. On the whole, though, Columbanus was following a "type" of the model spiritual life as it had developed in Celtic tradition—the wandering pilgrim for Christ. Over time, this ideal came to include itinerant preaching to non-Christians, but its primary focus was the imitation of Christ as a complete and ordered way of life.

Chapter 6
The Distant Islands Shall Rejoice
Expansion in Northern Europe

> **MAJOR FIGURES**
> - Patrick (Ireland)
> - Columba (Ireland & Scotland)
> - Augustine of Canterbury (England)
> - Paulinus (northern England)
> - Aidan (northern England)
> - Mungo/Kentigern (Scotland)
> - Gall, Amandus, and Kilian (Germany)
> - Egbert, Wilfrid, and Willibrord (Frisia)
> - Boniface (Germany)

In the history of early Christianity, there are only two periods in which missionary activity was so consistent and sustained as to deserve the title of "mission movement." One was the steady and spectacular growth of the Church of the East through Persia and central Asia, and another was the expansion of the Celtic church of Ireland and its heir, the Anglo-Saxon church. This Celtic/Anglo-Saxon wave has its genesis in the work of the famous Saint Patrick, but only takes its full shape later, when missionary-minded monastic founders like Columba and Columbanus took their Celtic Christianity back to Britain and continental Europe. Many Anglo-Saxon churches, influenced as much by the Celtic tradition from Iona and Lindisfarne as by the Roman tradition in Canterbury, carried on the heritage of missions well into the eighth century.

Ireland

> **ASPECTS OF EXPANSION**
> - Obedience to missionary commands in scripture
> - Monastic practices

To begin our survey of the Christianization of the British Isles, we must first turn back the clock a few centuries. Christianity had its birth in Britain well before the rule of Constantine, and possibly as early as the first century.

There are a few legends that Paul made it as far north as Britain in a missionary journey unrecorded in Scripture, but this is doubtful. The faith probably made its first entrance through Christian soldiers in the Roman army. The great English historian Bede tells us of the martyrdom of Alban in Britain, which occurred during the great persecution near the end of the third century (*Ecclesiastical History of the English People* 1.7). Other than that, we have very little knowledge of early Roman Christianity in Britain.

Nevertheless, this early faith took root among the native Britons, who preserved it even beyond the Anglo-Saxon invasions of the sixth century. And it was from this Romanized British stock that the isles brought forth their first great missionary: Patrick.

Historically speaking, we have only a shadowy caricature of Patrick's life. There still exists a *Confessio* reputed to be from his own hand, which is our main source of information. But much of his story is clouded by the legends that grew up from hagiographical biographies written several hundred years later. What we do know is this: that he was born into a British Christian family, that as a young man he was taken in captivity to Ireland for a period of six or seven years, and that at some point after escaping Ireland, he was convicted of a missionary calling to go back and share his faith with the island's inhabitants. We cannot date these events with certainty, but we do know that they fell within the fifth century.

Patrick's *Confessio* is astounding for its time—the reflections of a great man, so self-effacingly humble that his humility itself is winsome. He tells us little about the course of events in his ministry or of his methods of evangelism. But what he does tell us is directly valuable for the purposes of this study. As a defense of his ministry, he describes in detail his motivations for going to preach the gospel to the pagan Irish. First, he attributes his ministry to a specific, personal calling which he received in a vision. In that vision he was given a letter titled "The Voice of the Irish," and as he read it, he could hear the voices of those he had known in Ireland all calling out to him, "We beg you, holy boy, to come and walk again among us" (*Confessio* 23). Second, he has a deep affection for the Irish, praying that God should "never allow me to be separated from His people whom He has won in the ends of the earth" (58). Third, he lists gratitude and a sense of indebtedness as a motivation: "For after chastisement from God, and recognizing him, our way to repay him is to exalt him and confess his wonders before every nation under heaven" (3). And finally, he defends his missionary calling at length in terms of obedience to the specific commands of Scripture. He lists a number of passages, ending with the Great Commission itself (40). This is the first clear instance in which obedience to Scripture is listed as one of the primary motivations for missionary activity. As historian Richard Fletcher notes:

> Patrick's originality was that no one within western Christendom had thought such thoughts as these before, had ever previously been possessed by such convictions. As far as our evidence goes, he was the first person in Christian history to take the scriptural injunctions literally; to grasp that teaching all nations meant teaching even barbarians who lived beyond the frontiers of the Roman Empire.[1]

The fact that Patrick came to be regarded as the father of Irish Christianity is of no small importance; for the next three hundred years, the Irish would be the most active missionaries in western Christianity, and that missional impulse probably derived from the example of Patrick.

There were, undoubtedly, other early missionaries to the British Isles; unfortunately, we have only hints and shadows of them. We know of one Ninian, who evangelized among the Picts in southwest Scotland in the fifth century, and of Palladius, a bishop sent by Pope Celestine in 431 as "the first bishop to the Irish believers in Christ."[2] Palladius, who in some traditions was also known by the name of Patrick, presents two options to modern historians: either his mission encountered very little success, as a few traditions hold, or he was in fact one and the same Patrick as his more famous contemporary.[3] Beyond those speculations, our records fail us.

It is useful at this point to keep our focus on Ireland, because the gospel, having come over to Ireland from Britain, would soon be brought back to the larger island at the hands of Irish missionaries.

> *Within Ireland itself, evangelization proceeded mainly through monasticism.*

Within Ireland itself, evangelization proceeded mainly through monasticism. At this time, monasticism was a flexible movement, characterized by a wide diversity of rules, so each monastic founder was able to invent his own pattern. In Ireland, monasticism had its appeal in the ideal of a life of ascetic self-denial and in the way that it was able to accommodate the kinship and clientage structures of the surrounding culture.[4]

Between the time of Patrick and Columba, the sixth-century monastic founder par excellence (not to be confused with Columbanus, the missionary to the Franks), an individual ideal developed in Irish

---
1 Fletcher, *Barbarian Conversion*, 86.
2 Fletcher, 79–80.
3 Marnell, *Light from the West*, 16–17.
4 Fletcher, *Barbarian Conversion*, 91.

Christianity: that of the pilgrim. The monastic founders of the time were wanderers, establishing new monasteries as they went. Columba founded a number of monastic houses, including three that proved to be long-lasting and influential: Derry, Durrow, and Iona. Irish monasticism as a movement took on an ethos of communal pilgrimage, with new houses being planted on the margins of Christendom, where the message could diffuse out to the laity and then to the unevangelized beyond.[5]

Modern ideas of the missionary role fall somewhat short of comprehending the Irish pilgrim-monk. They were missionaries, but mission was not their only—sometimes not even their primary—goal. They certainly seemed more motivated by a genuine concern for the lost, and less by a militaristic practice of evangelism as spiritual warfare, than their forebears and contemporaries within the empire. Their main pursuit, however, was a driving ambition to imitate Jesus's manner of life in the gospels. If one were to pinpoint a scriptural linchpin to which their way of mission adhered, it would be in Jesus's instructions to his disciples when he sent them out to evangelize. Irish saints were missionaries, but they were missionaries by being pilgrims, by renouncing home to follow Christ at any cost. Mission was simply a part of the imitation of Christ.

Britain – England and Scotland

Aspects of Expansion
- Obedience to missionary commands in scripture
- Monastic practices

In the hundred years since Patrick's mission, the island of Britain suffered a massive and sustained invasion of pagan Germanic people groups. The Britons themselves were displaced toward Wales, while the Angles and Saxons took up residence in the areas that would come to be known as England. Into this situation, at the end of the sixth and beginning of the seventh centuries, two separate mission initiatives arose—the Roman mission to Canterbury and the Irish mission to Northumbria. From these two launch points, all of Britain's kingdoms were officially converted to Christianity, a process which took only a century.

For the mission to Canterbury, Bede's *Ecclesiastical History of the English People* is the main source. Bede, a careful historian and biblical scholar, lived in the monastery at Jarrow and wrote his magnum opus in 731, and it is marked

---
5 Fletcher, 94.

by diligent research and evenhanded evaluation. In Bede's account, the first protagonist of the Roman mission to Britain was Pope Gregory the Great. As the tale goes, Gregory (before ascending to the papacy) was walking through the marketplace in Rome and there saw some fair complexioned young captives for sale, and struck by their aspect, he asked the slave-seller where they came from. The man replied that they were from a pagan people called Angles, which to Gregory's ear sounded akin to "angels." Gregory was grieved by this encounter, exclaiming, "How sad that such bright-faced folk are still in the grasp of the author of darkness!" (*Eccl. Hist. of the English People* 2.1). From that point on, Gregory had it in mind to bring the gospel to the Angles. He implored the pope to send him as a missionary to Britain, but the people of Rome would not consent to the departure of their most beloved churchman.

It was not until Gregory himself was pope that his dream would be fulfilled. King Ethelbert of Kent (in southeastern England) married a Christian Frankish princess, Bertha, and it was to this couple that the first missionary team was sent. Gregory commissioned Augustine (named after the famous Augustine of Hippo) to go to Kent and preach the gospel there. Bede adds a story that informs our question of missionary motivations. Apparently Gregory was alone in his desire for missionaries to go to Britain, because Augustine himself, along with his companions, were not looking forward to the enterprise: "They became afraid, and began to consider returning home. For they were appalled at the idea of going to a barbarous, fierce, and pagan nation, of whose very language they were ignorant" (*Eccl. Hist. of the English People* 1.23). It was only Gregory's continued encouragement that prodded them on.

In considering Gregory's motivation for this effort, we see two main principles at work. First was a genuine concern for the Germanic peoples of Britain, especially after seeing the boys in the marketplace. It was not, however, a motivation shared by Gregory's forerunner in the papacy, by the missionary Augustine himself, or by anyone else in the story. Second, Gregory had a definite sense of empire, especially after his ascension to the papacy, an aspect of his thought that emerges from his other writings. He understood that the Roman Catholic Church was, in the wake of the barbarian invasions, the preserving influence that held together what once had been the western Roman Empire. And Britain was a part of that old empire.

Augustine's mission arrived in Canterbury (the capital of Kent) in 597 and was welcomed by King Ethelbert with great pomp. We know little of Augustine's missionary methods beyond that it included the establishment of a monastic settlement, but we do know that, even allowing for the possibility of inflated numbers, his mission was wildly successful. Bede makes it clear that he and his companions garnered respect for their holy manner of life. King Ethelbert consented to be baptized within the first few years of the mission, along with ten thousand of his people.[6] It is of no small importance that such a powerful king was among the first converts in Britain. Ethelbert used his influence to urge Christianity on his own people, and his choice carried great weight for surrounding kingships. Only a few years later, in 604, the East Saxons likewise accepted Christianity, which marked the beginning of the bishopric of London.[7]

The next major outreach of the Canterbury church was toward the powerful kingdom of Northumbria in northern England. King Edwin of Northumbria married the Christian daughter of Ethelbert of Kent, and Paulinus, one of Augustine's monks, traveled north as part of her retinue. According to Bede, this arrangement was undertaken on the agreement that Edwin would also become a Christian, for it was unfitting (at least in the Kentish view) for a Christian princess to marry a pagan. Paulinus, although his office as the new bishop of Northumbria consisted mainly of being a personal chaplain to the princess, immediately undertook to preach to the people of Northumbria. After some time, King Edwin pledged to Paulinus that he would accept baptism if God made him victorious in battle over his enemy, King Cuichelm of the West Saxons. He was indeed victorious, and so Edwin consented to become a Christian (*Eccl. Hist. of the English People* 2.9).

These two incidents are the central stories in the tale of the Anglo-Saxon kings converting to Christianity, and they are markedly similar to the conversion of Clovis. The common threads in all three stories are (1) the king being targeted as the chief convert, (2) the influence of a Christian wife, (3) a bishop as the active agent of evangelism, (4) a period of waiting and careful consideration on the part of the king, often including consultation with his chieftains, (5) the power of the new religion to bring victory in battle, and (6) the mass conversion of many of the people on the event of the king's baptism.

The last point mentioned raises the question of how sincere these mass conversions were. If Bede's account is correct, it would seem that these early conversions were more an act of loyalty to the king than a genuine heart-change on the part of the people. Eadbald, the son of King Ethelbert of Kent, was a pagan all his life, and when his father passed away, many in the kingdom took Eadbald's religious affiliation as an excuse to switch back to their old ways. The same thing happened in the kingdom of the East Saxons.

---

6 Cusack, *Rise of Christianity in Northern Europe*, 98.
7 Fletcher, *Barbarian Conversion*, 118–119.

When the initial convert, King Sabert, passed away in 616, his three pagan sons encouraged their people to return to the old gods. Bishop Mellitus of London was expelled from his see, and the apostasy was so great that even Laurence, the successor to Augustine in Canterbury, agreed that their best course of action was to abandon their dioceses and flee to Gaul (*Eccl. Hist. of the English People* 2.5). Some fifty years later, after a second evangelistic effort, the East Saxons fell into another mass apostasy during the course of a deadly plague (*Eccl. Hist. of the English People* 3.30). Historian D. H. Farmer sums up the process: "In several kingdoms the pattern was first, conversion of king and magnates, more or less shared by the rest of society, followed by apostasy and revival of paganism, and finally by a reconversion which proved permanent."[8]

Northumbria also suffered an apostasy after the death of King Edwin, followed by a period of strife among the royal houses. It was only resolved when the next Christian king, Oswald, arose. But Oswald brought a different sort of Christianity to Northumbria, which would define its course for the next hundred years. During his early life as a political exile, Oswald came to the faith through the ministry of Irish clerics in Scotland, and so it was Irish Christianity, rather than Roman, that he brought with him to the throne of Northumbria.[9]

From the island of Iona, off the west coast of Scotland, Columban monasticism spread into Britain. While the agents of mission for the Roman church were bishops, monastic founders and their monks served that purpose in the Irish church. Their influence spread north into Scotland and south into Northumbria. As noted earlier, Irish monasticism was a missional system whereby new houses were founded on the fringes of Christian territory. Those monasteries then became hubs of evangelism in the new area—a far cry from the common perception of monasticism as ineffective isolationism.

> While the agents of mission for the Roman church were bishops, monastic founders and their monks served that purpose in the Irish church.

Aidan, a monk from Iona, founded a monastery on the island of Lindisfarne, off the eastern coast of Scotland and Northumbria, and in the years that followed, Lindisfarne became the spiritual center of Irish

---

8 Farmer, "Notes," in Bede's *Ecclesiastical History*, 366.
9 Cusack, *Rise of Christianity in Northern Europe*, 106–7.

Christianity in Britain. Aidan and King Oswald worked together to reconvert Northumbria, with Aidan preaching and Oswald interpreting. For seven years, until Oswald's death, they carried on this preaching ministry to the Northumbrians, king and monk together, and their ministry bore great fruit.[10] With the support of Oswald and his court, Irish pilgrim-monks made deep inroads into northern England.

The influence of Irish monasticism provided a burst of new growth in English Christianity, as it had in Gaul, and it was Northumbrian missionaries that finished the evangelization of the last of the pagan English. The final kingdom to convert was Sussex (the South Saxons), along with the Isle of Wight, and both were evangelized by Wilfrid of Hexham, an exile from Northumbria. His ministry is worth noting because rather than focusing exclusively on the king and royal court, Wilfrid went first to the ordinary people, helping to alleviate a famine by teaching them fishing techniques. The people then, in sincere gratitude, listened to his preaching and accepted the faith.[11]

Even as the gospel was spreading throughout England, it was also taking root in Scotland. This could be expected, since the two fountainheads of the Celtic mission movement, Iona and Lindisfarne, sat astride opposite sides of the coast of Scotland. Columba himself is given credit for much of the initial work of evangelizing the Picts, some of the native inhabitants of Scotland. Along with twelve of his monks, he made contacts with noble Pict families, spreading the gospel and performing wonders that demonstrated the power of Christ. (Among these miracles was, allegedly, his act of banishing a mysterious water beast into the depths of Loch Ness.)

Other Celtic saints had a significant hand in the evangelization of Scotland, almost all of them monastic figures like Columba. One of these, Serf, was ministering to the Picts from a small abbey along the River Forth, when he became the protector of a young ward named Kentigern. Serf raised the boy, whom he nicknamed Mungo, imparting both his own faith and a passion for spreading the gospel through monastic witness. When Mungo was grown, he undertook a journey to one of the unevangelized provinces of western Scotland and became the founding saint of the city of Glasgow. He also made evangelistic tours of surrounding areas, including into Cumbria, in northwestern England. His influence was so immense that the traditions around him lavished him with titles like "Bishop of North Britain" (a post he never officially filled, to our knowledge) and "Chief Lord."[12]

---

10 Marnell, *Light from the West*, 57; Fletcher, *Barbarian Conversion*, 166.
11 Cusack, *Rise of Christianity in Northern Europe*, 108.
12 Davies, *Vanished Kingdoms*, 55.

Mungo's story, like those of so many Celtic missionaries, is replete with accounts of miracles that prove the power of Christ to the local populations. Beyond just the miracles, though, Mungo appears to have placed a significant emphasis on preaching the gospel. The motto attributed to him, still retained in the crest of the city of Glasgow, was "Let Glasgow flourish by the preaching of the Word!"[13]

Before we turn away from Britain, it is worth noting one last element that arises in Bede's account. During this long process of the evangelization of the Germanic arrivals in Britain, we must remember that the Welsh Britons had preserved their own ancient Christian heritage the whole time. However, being military and political enemies of the Anglo-Saxons, the Britons made no effort at evangelizing them. This in itself is no great surprise, but Bede takes exception to the Britons' isolationism: "Among the other unspeakable crimes ... they added this—that they never preached the Faith to the Saxons or Angles who dwelt with them in Britain" (*Eccl. Hist. of the English People* 1.22). What is remarkable is Bede's simple assumption that it is the duty of a Christian people to spread the gospel to the pagan people who live around them. It may seem like a natural assumption, but it only rarely appears in the texts of the first eight centuries of Christianity.

Germany and the Low Countries

Aspects of Expansion

- Evangelistic preaching
- Monastic practices
- Ecclesiastical organization
- Political affiliation
- Wandering pilgrims imitating Christ's mission instructions

Some four hundred years after the conversion of the Goths, a great number of Germanic tribes and kingdoms remained unconverted to Christianity. Some retained vestiges of the Arian faith, but others, like the Frisians and Danes, were entirely pagan. From the late seventh through the ninth century, the frontier of Christian missions in western Europe was in those areas that are now encompassed by modern Germany and the Low Countries. The groundwork of evangelization was laid by monks of the Columbanian diaspora—men like Gall, Amandus, and Kilian—Irish pilgrims who went out from Luxeuil and Bobbio to plant new mission-monasteries in Switzerland, southern Frisia (Belgium), and Thuringia (central Germany).

---

13 See Glass, *Mission of Saint Mungo*, 127–28.

Their ministry was based on the model of Columbanus, but beyond that, we know little of their work.

The conversion of Germany and the Low Countries, as it has been recorded for us in the chronicles of the time, falls along two main thrusts: the Anglo-Saxon missions to the continent, and the political campaigns of the Pippinid kingdom (the successors to Clovis's Merovingian dynasty in Gaul, and the precursors to Charlemagne's Carolingian empire).

The story of the Anglo-Saxon missions to the continent can be told as a tale of four interconnected ministries—those of Egbert, Wilfrid of Hexham (whom we mentioned above as the evangelist to Sussex), Willibrord, and Boniface—of whom the latter two are particularly important. Egbert and Wilfrid of Hexham were contemporaries, and both were Northumbrian exiles. Wilfrid appears to have been in exile because he was a controversial and contumacious churchman, whereas Egbert was a *peregrinus*—a pilgrim in the old Irish mold, who voluntarily renounced the comforts of home to live in the "white martyrdom" of pilgrimage and exile. He spent much of his life in Ireland, but he was the visionary leader of the Anglo-Saxon mission. Willibrord forms the connection between these two men—he was the foremost protégé of Egbert in Ireland, and he also lived in a monastery under Wilfrid's leadership for a time. Boniface came into the picture later on, eventually partnering with Willibrord's ministry in Frisia.

These were not the only Anglo-Saxon missionaries to go to Germany during this time; but they are the ones who left the greatest impact. Bede mentions another—Wictbert—who went to Frisia to preach the gospel and remained there for two years, but with no converts (*Eccl. Hist. of the English People* 5.9). He also tells us of Hewald the White and Hewald the Black, two more Anglo-Saxon priests in the Irish pilgrim mold, both of whom were martyred by the Frisians (5.10).

We begin, then, with Egbert. The passage in which Bede describes him is worth repeating in full, because it bears directly on our question of missionary motivations:

> He planned to bring blessings to more people by undertaking the apostolic work of preaching the word of God to some of the nations who had not heard it. He had learned that there were many such nations in Germany, of whose stock came the Angles and Saxons now settled in Britain .... These nations include the Frisians, Rugians, Danes, Huns, Old Saxons, and Boructuars besides many other races in that region who still observe pagan rites. So this warrior of Christ planned to sail around Britain and attempt to snatch some of them from Satan and bring them to Christ. (*Eccl. Hist. of the English People* 5.9)

Egbert's driving motive, then, beyond a simple concern for the lost, was the fact that these unevangelized Germans were his own kin. There was a familial affection between these peoples, much as there was between the Gothic tribes during the spread of Arian Christianity. The Frisians were related to the Germanic stock that had settled in England, and their languages remained close. Old English and Old Frisian were very similar, and at that time they may have been mutually intelligible dialects, which would have enabled the missionaries to preach in their native tongue.

Egbert himself, however, was unable to go. He was warned away from the attempt by a series of visions. Nevertheless, he pressed forward, only to have the ship on which he planned to sail wrecked in a terrible storm. So he remained in Ireland, but his vision for the conversion of the continental Germans was actively passed on to his disciples: "He still attempted to send other holy and zealous men for the work of preaching, among whom the outstanding figure by his priestly rank and his merit was one named Willibrord" (*Eccl. Hist. of the English People* 5.10).

But Wilfrid of Hexham was the first major Anglo-Saxon missionary to set foot in Frisia, on his way to Rome to plead a grievance before the pope. He stayed in Frisia over the whole winter of 678–79, having discovered there "a multitude of heathen," and he had some initial success there before resuming his journey to Rome when spring came.[14] Wilfrid's sojourn among the Frisians was not without lasting impact, because word of his efforts came back to the network of monks connected to the Abbey of Ripon, where Wilfrid had served as abbot. Among those monks was the thirty-three-year-old priest Willibrord, the disciple of Egbert.

> *Christianity is not to be lived only for oneself, but also for the benefit of others.*

Alcuin, his biographer, gives us some hint of Willibrord's motivation at this juncture: "The fervor of his faith had reached such an intensity that he considered it of little value to labor at his own sanctification unless he could preach the Gospel to others and bring some benefit to them. He had heard that in the northern regions of the world the harvest was great but the laborers few" (*Life of Willibrord* 5). In this statement, we have an explicit appeal to Scripture, as well as the realization that Christianity is not to be lived only for oneself, but also for the benefit of others. This matches the Irish understanding of pilgrimage and the imitation of Christ as a whole way of living, one that ministers both to one's own soul and to those one meets along the way.

---

14 Duckett, *Wandering Saints*, 178.

Willibrord arrived in Frisia during a tumultuous time. The king of Frisia, Radbod, was trying to free himself from the imperialist ambitions of Pippin II, a Frankish king, and he was hostile to Willibrord's attempts to preach the gospel. The work was slow at first, and Willibrord decided to move on from Frisia and go to Denmark, since the Danes were another of the kinship-peoples that Egbert had targeted. This was a courageous act: whereas the Frisians were at least within the power sphere of the Christian Franks, Denmark was deep beyond the frontier, far removed from any help or support. The Danes proved just as hostile as the Frisians and wanted nothing of Willibrord and his message. So Willibrord bought thirty young men as slaves and took them back with the intention of freeing them, training them in the faith, and sending them back to Denmark as missionaries.[15]

Eventually the politics in Frisia calmed, and Willibrord, who in the meantime had received papal approval for the mission, returned to begin a ministry based in the city of Utrecht. He was installed as bishop there, and he proceeded to preach in the surrounding towns and villages, gradually winning more and more of the Frisians to the faith. It was still difficult work, made more so by the lingering hostility of King Radbod. Willibrord's ministry was given security and stability by its support from the Frankish Pippinid rulers, but their backing also made Willibrord's message a hard sell to Radbod and his people, who resented the Pippinids as unjust conquerors.[16]

Into this world stepped the largest figure of all: Boniface. In 716, after a distinguished early career as one of the finest and most respected scholar-teachers in England, he sailed for Frisia. His main biographer, Willibald, gives us little hint as to his missionary motivation, but one gets the impression that his desire to go to Frisia fell within the paradigm of the *peregrinus*, the Irish-Christian pilgrim. However, as in Willibrord's first arrival in Frisia, he found the area in turmoil and surmised that no work could yet be accomplished. So he turned around, but his heart never left Frisia. Willibald tells us that on that first visit, "he decided that if at any time he could see his way to approach the people, he would [return to] minister to them the Word of God" (*Life of St. Boniface* 4).

In May of 719 he received a formal commission from the pope to undertake the evangelization of Germany. He returned to Frisia, and there he partnered with Willibrord for three years in the ministries of preaching and teaching. This was immediately after the death of Radbod, and Willibald tells us that Boniface was able to reach "districts that had hitherto been left untouched by the preaching of the Gospel .... The results of this work, so close

---

15 Fletcher, *Barbarian Conversion*, 201.
16 Cusack, *Rise of Christianity in Northern Europe*, 122.

to his heart, were swift and spontaneous .... . He destroyed pagan temples and shrines, built churches and chapels, and with the help of Willibrord gained numerous converts to the church" (*Life of St. Boniface* 5).

After his ministry internship under Willibrord, he set off for the largely unreached regions of central Germany, where his ministry was to take root. He preached throughout the regions of Hesse and Thuringia, converting both kings and the ordinary folk. After a long ministry of building up the church in central Germany, he returned to the mission field he loved—Frisia—and was martyred there.

Boniface is first and foremost remembered as a missionary, but his greatest work was in organizing the new German church and reforming the neighboring Frankish church. He assaulted the laxity of Frankish clergy and reinstated the ancient practice of annual church synods. His great passion was for evangelism, and he seems to have been genuinely shocked and puzzled that the Frankish clerics did not share that ambition. This is worth noting, because his ministry came to connect ecclesiastical reform and power-consolidation with the task of evangelism, which became one of the foundational principles of the later Carolingian renaissance.[17] He was unpopular at first among the clerics around him, but by the end of his life he was the most well-known and revered churchman in all of Gaul or Germany. A few other Anglo-Saxon missionaries, such as Bishop Lull, carried on after Boniface's death and consolidated his gains.

Missionary Motivations

With Celtic and Anglo-Saxon churches, we come to one of the high points in the story of early Christian mission. Patrick, the founding figure of this mission movement, appears to be one of the first Christians since the apostolic age to take the Great Commission passages seriously and apply them to his own context. Other biblical inspirations for mission were plentiful, as we have seen: Christians were motivated by the grand prophetic vision of Malachi 1:11, wherein they saw themselves as the fulfillment of all nations bringing pure sacrifices to God (see ch. 8 below); and some parts of early Christianity took Jesus's mission instructions in Luke 10 as their paradigm. The Great Commission texts, however, such as Matthew 28:18–20 or Acts 1:8, make almost no appearance as a motivation for mission until Patrick's time.

Patrick also shows sincere compassion, a sense of concern for those who do not yet know the way of Christ. In his case, however, as in others, this compassion is grounded in a previously existing sense of kinship with the

---

17 Fletcher, *Barbarian Conversion*, 209.

people to whom he goes. While not closely related to the Irish in an ethnic/cultural sense, Patrick's early experiences meant that he knew the Irish language and society on an intimate basis before embarking on his mission to them. Similarly, the compassion demonstrated in the accounts of Anglo-Saxon missionaries to Frisia and Germany is magnified by a sense of ethnic kinship. Nonetheless, it is in the Celtic mission movement that we first find a clear and consistent articulation of mission being undertaken for the sake of the other. Themes of the reign of Christ are no doubt still present, but do not feature as large here as within the Roman Empire or the eastward expansion of the church.

The Celtic mission movement also highlights yet another aspect of early missionary motivations: the desire to imitate the way of Christ. Perhaps more than any other factor, this desire shaped and drove the pattern of Celtic and Anglo-Saxon missions. Like other mission movements inspired by the idea of a wandering monastic lifestyle (such as in the early Christian expansion in east Syria and Mesopotamia), Celtic monasticism had as one of its expressions the idea of "white martyrdom"—living as a pilgrim who wanders the world, forsaking home for the sake of Christ. It was an attempt to live as Christ and the disciples lived, walking from place to place, living a life of prayer and devotion, and representing the holiness and love of the Christian life to all those you met on the way. Evangelism was certainly a major part of this ideal, but only one part among many. It was conceived as a fully orbed way to live the ideal Christian life, conforming as close as possible to the life of Jesus in the gospels.

> *It was an attempt to live as Christ and the disciples lived.*

Chapter 7
The Mission of the Kingdom
Communal Aspects of Missionary Motivation

Having completed our survey of early Christian missions, we have the opportunity now to draw some deductions from the shape of the data. The crucial question is this: *What does mission look like when undertaken in the spirit of early Christianity?* It is impossible to give just a single answer to that question, since early Christianity was a widespread movement with significant local and historical variations, but some broad outlines emerge. As we have seen, mission movements in early Christianity tended to be communal and ecclesial in aspect, driven not so much by a desired result as by a theological vision. Concepts of ecclesial and individual identity, rather than goals to be achieved, determined the shape of early Christian mission.

The Ecclesiastical Model

First, we can say that mission in the spirit of early Christianity is *communal* and *ecclesial*. As the historian of mission Edward Smither notes, "One defining attribute of early Christian mission was that the church itself was a viable locus of mission."[1] Not only were churches practical hubs for the extension of further missions, but they also represented, in and of themselves, one of the great goals of early Christian mission. Such missions did not seem to have the salvation of individuals as their primary goal (though that is of course assumed), but the establishment of communities of faith. The missionary outgrowth of the early church happened in concert with the establishment and development of ecclesiastical order, which by the second century had already begun to take on a pattern of bishoprics and dioceses. These terms should not, however, spark images of great cathedrals, parish churches, and men in liturgical robes—such things were later features of ecclesiastical networks.

In the second and third centuries, these networks were marked not by basilicas and clerical mitres but by relationships between people. The networks were organized around the development of the threefold orders of *episkopoi* (bishops/overseers), *presbyteroi* (pastors/priests), and *diakonoi* (deacons), and the communities they represented. Missionary outreaches into the rural

---

[1] Smither, *Mission in the Early Church*, 159.

hinterlands were typically organized on this model of ecclesiastical networks, often by sending out a wandering bishop (*chorepiscopos*) to evangelize, organize, and administer a new region. By the fourth, fifth, and sixth centuries, other communal networks—like monasticism—also emerged, adding further dynamic communities for missional expansion.

The fundamental point to grasp here is that there was a unanimous assumption that missional activity was centered on bringing forth *communities* of faith that would be immediately plugged into the broader structure of the global church. Although one-on-one personal witnessing certainly happened, as some testimonies from the early church relate, the intentional models of cross-cultural mission did not adopt "personal evangelism" as a methodology. The goal was not to so much to save individuals as to establish new local churches or monastic communities. It was the community of faith that was considered the central incarnation of the reign of Christ, and so it was the establishment of new communities that took on preeminent importance.

To say that mission ought to be focused on establishing communities of faith should come as no surprise; even those models which aim at the salvation of individuals usually conceive of an indigenous local church as part of the end goal. But the distinction runs deeper than it appears at first glance. In the view of early Christianity, a local community of faith represented more than just a collection of individuals who gathered for worship and mutual edification. Rather, the community constituted a new incarnation of the reality of the reign of Christ, holding a metaphysical value of its own as a *sacramentum*—a holy mystery that represents and instantiates the new order which is breaking into the world.[2] As the church father Cyprian wrote, "Thus also the church, when the light of the Lord is poured forth, ... sheds her rays of light throughout the whole world."[3] A gathered community of faith was an instance of the messianic reign irrupting into new cultures and locations, and thus much more than just a collection of individuals united by common convictions.

> *A gathered community of faith was an instance of the messianic reign irrupting into new cultures and locations.*

The communality of the local church was itself an important part of the sacramental nature of church: by submitting to one another in love, and further, by submitting to the officers of the church, connected as they were to

---

2 See Clément, *Roots of Christian Mysticism*, 95.
3 Quoted in Sittser, *Resilient Faith*, 111.

the network of the universal church, each local church joined the universal submission of the saints to the reign of Christ in a direct and concrete way. An individual believer simply could not represent this aspect of the reign of Christ in the same way that a community of faith could, and thus the community was the primary goal.

The value of the gathered community of faith was not just in its communality, but also in its worship. If the universal mutual submission of believers to one another was one of the characteristic manifestations of Christ's reign, their collective worship was another. Early Christians appear to have considered the church as an eschatological sign—a physical, in-history appearance of the dawning age of the messianic reign. Christ reigns now, but that reign is still to be manifested in a full, final, and universal way in the future. The church is both the primary representation of Christ's present, heavenly reign, as well as the signpost pointing toward the coming fullness of his universal reign.

The collective worship of the church is one of the main ways in which the church's calling as an eschatological sign is expressed. Following on Jewish ideas of temple worship, the liturgy of early Christians was considered an actual participation in heavenly realities. It wasn't just that Christians were directing their worship to God, it was that their union with Christ in the Spirit transformed the communal gathering of Christians into an actual participation in the presence of God. When Christians gather to worship, they are conceived to be joining the eternal service of worship around the throne of God, anchoring their local practice in an event that is beyond all space and time. The worship of the church expresses the worship of heaven and reflects that reality into the timebound experience of earth: an entrance into the kingdom itself, centered on the Lamb upon the throne and surrounded by the praise of all creation.

This focus on the gathered worship of Christians as the goal of mission is based on Old Testament prophecies of the messianic reign. In texts like Isaiah 2:2–3 and Malachi 1:11, the coming age is marked by the global worship of all nations. Early Christians saw themselves as the fulfillment of these prophecies. Thus, simply by raising their pure sacrifices of praise and thanksgiving from many different lands, early Christians believed they were enacting a literal fulfillment of God's plan for the world. If one was to identify a primary goal of early Christian mission, it would likely be along those lines: the establishment of the worship of the one true God in every nation under heaven, in fulfillment of prophecy and in anticipation of the coming fullness of the kingdom.

If that is indeed what church is—an irreplaceable instantiation of the kingdom of God, breaking into the world and pointing to the dawning fullness of Christ's reign—then the early Christian sensibility of aiming at the establishment of communities of faith, as a primary rather than secondary goal, becomes understandable. The value of church exceeds the benefits it gives to individual believers; it constitutes something, in and of itself, which is of such immense value in the plan of God as to be a primary concern of Christian mission. The whole is greater than the sum of its parts.

This communal and ecclesial methodology is deeply rooted in New Testament practice. Paul's letters make it clear that his mission was not simply to convert individuals here and there to belief in Jesus, but to establish communities of faith everywhere he went. The communal aspect was central to his vision of what the plan of God in Christ was all about. God's plan, as told by Paul, was a mission of cosmic reconciliation—bringing all things together in heaven

> *By raising their pure sacrifices of praise and thanksgiving, early Christians believed they were enacting a literal fulfillment of God's plan for the world.*

and on earth under Christ—and the "bringing together" aspect of local church life was one of the main ways in which that reconciliation was being worked out. Thus the mission of God in the world will always include the bringing together of disparate individuals into a mutual submission of love. It extends to include the bringing together of people from different races, cultures, and languages into one common worship before the throne of God. Reconciliation is at the heart of the mission of God, and its primary expression is in the church.

The Monastic Model

While the organization of new churches, dioceses, and episcopal territories was often the way missions progressed in early Christianity, the local church was not the only communal expression of the faith to grow from those movements. Monasticism also played a critical role in many early mission movements, such that monasteries (or other monastic-style communities) often became the most visible communal expression of the faith in new areas.[4] According to the eminent historian Peter Brown, monasticism was perhaps the greatest single factor in the expansion of Christianity during the late antique period: "It was paradoxically just these eccentrics [i.e., monks] who turned Christianity into a mass religion. They did this largely through their ability to sum up, in their persons, the piety of the average Roman now turned Christian."[5]

---

4 See Smither, *Mission in the Early Church*, 39–43.
5 Brown, *World of Late Antiquity*, 107.

Most prominent in the monastic-style expansion of the faith were the mission movements in the Celtic sphere of influence and in the Church of the East. The Celtic model, especially as pioneered by Columba and Columbanus, focused on planting cenobitic (communal) monasteries in new areas. These monasteries would then become missional hubs for evangelism, discipleship, and outreach, as the monks interacted with neighboring villages. Monasteries would offer services of worship for the area and would receive requests to pray for community members. Its leaders (who felt they needed extra prayers because of the violent nature of their political offices), as well as the sick and infirm, would be drawn to these offers of prayer. Gradually, new local recruits would join the monastery until it was large enough to send out teams of monks to plant new monasteries further out into the frontiers, and the pattern would repeat itself. In this way, Celtic monasticism succeeded in planting missional communities across the landscape of northwestern Europe.

In the Church of the East's sphere of influence a similar picture unfolded, though the monastic structure was of a different sort. The monastic heritage received in the east also included *cenobiticism* (large communal monasteries), but its main thrust was eremitic, based around the monastic labors of hermits, either singly or in small groups. The first waves of these movements, particularly in Syrian Christianity, appear to have been modeled directly upon Jesus's practice of sending out mission workers in pairs on ascetical journeys of preaching. The first evangelists of east Syria and Mesopotamia—men like Addai and Aggai—were said to have followed that model. It caught on in Persia, where the wandering-pilgrim model of monasticism, represented in the "Sons and Daughters of the Covenant," became one of the early expressions of Persian Christianity.

Another of the earliest monastic models was that of the desert anchorites, who chose a spot in the wilderness and stayed there indefinitely (another form of eremitic monasticism). Such patterns emerged contemporaneously in Egypt, Palestine, and western Syria, where figures like Antony the Great and Simon Stylites became famous for their ascetic devotion. Missionary outreach was not the primary goal of these hermits, but it was very often the result. Their holiness of life, which according to the sources often included the ability to perform miracles, led to significant local fame. As Philip Jenkins writes, "The best argument for Christianity was that its holy men and women were so close to God that they could defy the laws of nature and demonstrate divine power through acts of miracle and healing."[6]

---

6 Jenkins, *Lost History of Christianity*, 76.

The pattern often went as follows: first, a hermit would take up residence in one of the marginal areas, in or near the wilderness. In most of the east (unlike in Egypt), the wilderness was not an uninhabited wasteland; it was often just over the crest of the hill from the nearest village, standing amid local populations.[7] Soon reports of a holy man living nearby would pass through the villages of the area, sparking both curious gawkers and sincere spiritual seekers to come and see the hermits. In most cases, then, the hermits did not find uninterrupted solitude, but rather a stream of people coming out to request prayers for themselves or to ask questions of spiritual counsel. So great was the influence some of them wielded that they often found themselves being consulted by officials and churchmen, who sought their opinions on matters of theology and sectarian differences.[8]

> **Missionary outreach was not the primary goal of these hermits, but it was very often the result.**

The presence of a hermit would often spark a movement of lay devotion in the area, including the conversion of some formerly pagan onlookers who were so impressed by the hermit's piety that they put their faith in Christ. In some cases, the hermits (who usually really did want to find some solitude) would leave their pillars and caves and go somewhere further out into the wilderness, and the result was that they kept pressing outward into the territories of frontier peoples where the gospel had not yet taken root. These people were no less curious about the strange holy men in their midst, so they would come out to observe the hermits and ask about their way of life, and the whole process would begin again.

In some parts of the east, a hybrid model between cenobitic and eremitic monasticism took hold, in which hermits would band together to form a *laura*—a network of individual retreats scattered across a broad area, from which they would gather together once a week for worship and the sharing of a common life. As was the case with Celtic monasticism, when a particular community got too full of new recruits to be manageable, the leaders would send some of them off further into the wilderness to plant a new *laura*, thus pressing the influence of the communities ever outward.[9]

In the monastic-mission model, as with the ecclesiastical-mission model, the idea of the worshiping community was central. Those who went out on mission did so not just to make converts, but primarily to establish

---

7 Brown, "Rise and Function of the Holy," 83.
8 Potter, *Roman Empire at Bay*, 490.
9 Binns, "Introduction," in *Cyril of Scythopolis*, xvi–xix.

a kingdom-oriented way of life in a place that did not yet have it. Missional monasticism was motivated as much (if not more) by a sense of obedience to the vision of Malachi 1:11—of worship rising to God from all nations—than to the words of Christ in the Great Commission.

> *Those who went out on mission did so not just to make converts, but primarily to establish a kingdom-oriented way of life in a place that did not yet have it.*

The hermits and monks went out into the wilderness, finding places beyond the frontiers and establishing outposts from which the sacrifice of praise and prayer could rise perpetually before the throne of God. The result, inevitably, was the spread of the gospel, though preaching and proclamation were not usually among the primary motivations for going. When the Celtic monastic movement expanded out of Ireland, they sought out-of-the-way places like the islands of Iona and Lindisfarne. At first glance, the selection of obscure locales would seem to diminish the possibilities of Christian expansion, and yet this monastic diaspora to the frontiers became the linchpin of a great wave of evangelization in Britain.

In the case of eremitic monks (hermits), there was often a territorial notion of spiritual warfare involved in their travels—going into the deserts, which were thought to be a bastion of retreating demonic powers, in order to confront the powers there.[10] The result of their labor was missional in a way that was not limited to spiritual warfare alone: local villagers in those sparsely populated areas sought them out for prayer and counsel; other monks came out to join them; and the stories of their holiness were brought back and circulated throughout the Christian world, inspiring many more to similar lifestyles of devotion.

While the Celtic and eastern forms of monasticism were missionally oriented, at least in the sense of pushing ever outward into frontier areas, other forms of monasticism were just as important in helping previously evangelized areas retain a foothold in the faith even when many other social factors were pushing back against Christianity. The spread of Benedictine monasticism in southern and western Europe, for example, left a solid, self-perpetuating foundation for local, communal expressions of Christianity to persist, even in the face of continuing invasions from Germanic tribes in the north and Islamic expansion in the south. Throughout massive social upheavals and challenges to the faith from both non-Christians and heretical groups, monasticism's focus on a disciplined life of holiness proved difficult

---
10 Hall, *Worshiping with the Church Fathers*, 231.

to erode, and its persistence allowed it to remain a winsome and compelling vision of Christian practice in the midst of difficult times.

In every case of monastic expansion, the primary goal was the same: to create outposts where the life of the in-breaking kingdom of God could be manifested and practiced in a direct and disciplined way. The importance of an ongoing cycle of worship—and especially of communal worship—was at the heart of the monastic life. Even solo hermits were often advised in monastic literature to remember that their devotional rhythm of life was not based on their own habits alone, but was part of the grander rhythm of prayer and praise being raised by Christian communities all over the world. In one anecdote recorded by Athanasius, a hermit who has grown proud of his personal prayer life is admonished in a vision and called to recognize the surpassing power of communal prayer:

> *The importance of an ongoing cycle of worship was at the heart of the monastic life.*

> They used to tell of a certain monk ... that although he kept frequent vigil and prayed, he was neglectful about joining with the congregation in prayer. And one night there appeared to his gaze a glorious pillar of brilliant light, rising from the place where the congregation had gathered; and it reached to the heavens. Then he saw a small spark, which [flew separately] about the pillar, and sometimes it shone brightly, but sometimes it was extinguished. And while he was wondering about the vision, it was explained to him by God, who said, "The pillar which you see is the prayers of the many who are gathered together .... And the spark is the prayers of those ... who despise the appointed services of the congregation. So now, if you would live, perform that which is customary to perform with the congregation, and only then, if you ... are able to pray separately, do so." (*Paradise of the Holy Fathers* 2.135)

This vision, of prayer rising before the throne of God, shows the power of the early Christian conception of communal worship. The worship of the people of God, wherever it was happening in the world, offered a direct connection to the timeless, unchangeable reality of God's own presence. In essence, it created a union between the physical places of our world and the divine dwelling, beyond space and time in the heavenlies. Part of the early Christian conception of mission was that this vision of communal worship should include the whole earth, thus fulfilling Paul's summation of God's great plan in Christ: "to unite all things in him, things in heaven and things in earth" (Eph 1:10).

The Peregrine Model

The focus on community as an aspect of mission goes all the way back to Jesus sending out his disciples to proclaim the kingdom as part of his Galilean ministry. Jesus sent his disciples out *in community* and *to communities*. According to the gospels, Jesus sent them out two by two (Mark 6:7), with instructions to go into towns and make contact with households that would receive them. Once received into a household, they were told not to move around to other houses in the town, but to stay there until their preaching and healing in the town was complete (Mark 6:10; Luke 10:7).

Consider the fact that there were alternatives which Jesus could have employed. He could have sent the disciples out singly rather than in groups. Further, since he was encouraging them to a lifestyle of ascetic wandering (no bread, no bag, no money, no extra clothes), he certainly could have instructed them to find a cave or a tent or to sleep under a tree for their shelter. Instead, he puts them in communities and sends them to communities. The specific command to stay in the house that receives them, rather than moving around, shows an intentionality toward building community in the places they go. They are not simply seeking shelter or hospitality; they are there to build relationships and invest in the spiritual life of an entire household. When they move on to the next town, that household will remain, the locus of a new expression of kingdom-life in the midst of the wider community.

This community-building style of evangelism carried over to the apostolic missions, as can be seen in the work of Paul's ministry teams in the book of Acts. Although the missional expansion of early Christianity sometimes happened by way of a single individual (as by the witness of a captive or a rural bishop's wandering ministry), the more common pattern is that mission occurred in communities and to communities. The Church of the East copied the method of Jesus's instructions for generations, and others adapted them to local conditions. In Celtic monasticism, the idea of becoming a *peregrinus*—a wanderer in the mold of Jesus's emissaries—became one of the highest ideals of the spiritual life, comparable to martyrdom. And in each set of peregrines that went out, the promise of Jesus was held central—that where two or more are gathered in his name, there he is too. The community of faith was at center stage, even in the two-by-two wanderings of peregrine monks.

The Primary Value of Worshiping Communities

In every case, there was an emphasis not just on getting individual souls to repent, but on building up worshiping communities through the message of God's kingdom. Later Protestant conceptions of mission also held the establishment of worshiping communities as an end goal of the mission, but the method was rather different. The missionaries who formed the leading edge of the great Protestant mission movement would go out to a new area in the hope of making enough converts to then draw together into a church. In their conception, the making of converts preceded the establishment of a worshiping community.

In the common pattern of early Christian mission, however, that process is reversed. Mission was usually undertaken by planting a worshiping community, which would then serve as a center of gravity for winning converts. Although there were individual missions which proved the exception to the rule, the normal pattern was for an established community of faith, or a representative thereof, to go out and establish a pattern of worship. A group of monks would go and start a new monastery; wandering peregrines going about in pairs would set up temporary hermitages from which to practice their devotional offices; rural bishops would look for a good location from which to offer church services as an extension of the nearby diocese; and clerical missions to royal courts would begin by establishing a cycle of worship among their own clergy as soon as they were planted in their new home.

> *Worship was not simply an aftereffect of conversion, it was one of the main purposes for which Christians existed.*

The establishment of a cycle of worship by the newly arrived community of faith was the first order of business, and from that center, the work of the kingdom could proceed. Whether it was a monastery doing its devotional offices or a cleric performing the rituals of a church service, the impact of the order of worship would ripple out into surrounding communities. Worship was not simply an aftereffect of conversion, a helpful spiritual discipline for the edification of Christians; it was one of the main purposes for which Christians existed.[11] Worship was *leitourgia* (liturgy), which in Greek means "the work of the people." It was a high calling and a necessary prerogative of Christian identity. Since early Christians essentially believed that the local meeting of the Body of Christ for worship was an event in which spiritual realities were made manifest, in which heaven and earth were united, and in which people could enter fully into the duties for which they were created, the worship of the community took on a gravity that drew people in.

---

11 See Sittser, *Resilient Faith*, 121.

The central vision of early Christianity was that Christ the King was on his throne, and that all people could now participate in the advance of his kingdom by repenting, pledging their allegiance to him in faith, and joining in the endless cycle of worship around his throne. Converts did not come to Christianity just so that they could join that vision of heavenly worship in the distant future of the afterlife, but so that they could join it immediately, in the context of the community's worship. Entrance into the kingdom was a present reality, given in worship as a foretaste of what was to come, and the worship of the church was considered a real participation in the worship around Christ's throne in heaven. Thus it was by worship that each local instantiation of the kingdom took root, and it was worship that formed the first step in any mission endeavor.

Chapter 8
Emissaries of the King
Individual Aspects of Missionary Motivation

Having considered the communal dimensions of early Christian mission in the previous chapter, we now turn our attention to the individual dimension. As we've seen, mission in early Christianity was usually done *in community* and *to communities*. However, this doesn't mean that individual dimensions had no part to play. Much of the missional activity of early Christianity was motivated by a particular understanding of Christian identity. This individual dimension thus represents not the goal of missional activity, but one's sense of personal motivation for mission.

Officers of the Kingdom

The first point to consider comes when we look at Jesus's own proclamation, repeated many times in the gospels: "The kingdom of God is at hand!" New Testament scholars have made tremendous advances in the past half-century in helping modern audiences understand this message in its original context, but one aspect often goes unnoticed. When modern audiences read "the kingdom of God," they tend to view it as an abstraction: either as a metaphor for God's universal providence or as a future state, a way of describing the eschatological reality that was breaking into history through Jesus's life, death, and ministry. While such notions are not untrue, they do miss the fact that in the ancient world, a "kingdom" (or more properly, a "reign") was not an abstraction. It was something very practical, this-world, able to be seen and touched and directly experienced in one's daily life.

People in the ancient world thought about reigns as we might think about a political administration or form of government. Just as we can point to features of governmental administration all around us, from city councils to police officers to the currency we use, so people in Jesus's day saw and experienced the reign of the Romans and Herodians in a multitude of practical forms. Roman garrisons sat beside road junctions, tax collectors manned their booths, and Herod's builders raised monuments of his administration all around the country. While words like "kingdom" and "reign" could have a broader application in the more general sense of "sovereignty," it was commonly also a very practical thing, touching the fabric of daily life and the passage of ordinary time. Some early Christian documents referred to the global Christian community as a commonwealth (*oikoumene*)—a practical, political term which the Roman Empire also applied to itself.[1]

The practical nature of the kingdom of God can also be seen earlier in Israel's history, in the controversy during Samuel's time about the people's request for a king. If God's reign had merely been something abstract or future oriented, a way of speaking about general providence, then having an earthly king would be no infringement upon the kingdom of God. The story, however, clearly shows that it was an infringement—the earthly kingship they requested amounted to a tacit rejection of God's kingship over them (1 Sam 8:6–7). This implies that the reign of God was not something abstract or merely spiritual, but a very real aspect of Israelites' daily lives, a sovereign administration tended by God's chosen officers of priests, judges, and prophets.

So also with Jesus's proclamation: while it certainly does speak of God's providence and of eschatological realities, we must also recognize that Jesus's audience probably would have heard it as something practical. People counted the passing years with reference to the reigning emperor, so when Jesus showed up in (or around) the fifteenth year of the reign of Tiberius and proclaimed instead the reign of God, it would have sounded like something real, practical, and substantive was on its way. A reign had officers and outposts; it had boots on the ground. This is why Jesus's message was so often taken by his opponents as a political message, a call for a revolution against Rome's authority.

Jesus, however, consistently denied the interpretation that his proclamation of the kingdom was political. As he clarified to Pontius Pilate, his kingdom was "not of this world" (John 18:36). Yet he also made it clear that even though his movement was not *of* the world, it was absolutely to be present *in* the world (John 17:14–18). It would not array itself in the aspects of power, violence, or coercive authority that marked human reigns; it would not seek to launch wars or conquer earthly powers; but it would nevertheless be present in the midst of human dominions, spreading like yeast through dough.[2] As the east Syrian writer Bardaisan explained it, the people of Christ might be living under the laws of many different kingdoms throughout the world, but they only bowed the knee to one set of laws—the law of the Messiah.[3]

This presence of Christ's kingdom in the world would, like all reigns, be administered through its officers. Jesus clearly intended for his movement

---

[1] Sittser, *Resilient Faith*, 109.

[2] See Sittser, *Resilient Faith*, 102.

[3] Brown, *Rise of Western Christendom*, 40.

> *This presence of Christ's kingdom in the world would, like all reigns, be administered through its officers.*

to be incarnated in the offices endowed on his followers. He selected twelve disciples and commissioned them as his apostles (his "sent-out ones")—not a typical practice for a Jewish rabbi of his day. Further, he endowed them with his own authority and gave them particular tasks for evangelism, discipleship, and tending his flock of followers. As the early church grew, it developed around specific roles and offices, from apostles and deacons to presbyters and overseers. The reign of Christ had begun, and it was visible, in a partial and incipient way, in the church and its officers. Local congregations were the embassy outposts from which Christ's ambassadors served in the midst of earthly dominions. One day the kingdom would come in its fullness, in which Christ would reign with his saints, but a glimpse of that future was already taking shape in the covenant communities of the Christian faith.

Royal Priesthood

Within early Christianity, offices were not only assigned to those filling roles in the church's institutions, but (at least informally) to all members of the church as well. Christians were placed back in the old roles of ancient Israel—and even further back, of Adam and Eve—as God's "royal priesthood," "kings and priests," the ones who ruled creation and tended the sanctuary.[4]

The earliest baptismal liturgies reflect roots that run back to the consecration ceremonies for Jewish priests. Initiation to the Jewish priesthood included a full-body ceremonial washing, an anointing with oil, and the robing of the priest in the garments of his new role. Christian baptisms included the same three elements. First came the washing, which was the baptism itself. In Jewish tradition, the washing for priestly initiation was to be done with "living water"—water that moved and brought life: streams, rivers, or ritual mikvehs. Christian customs followed the same practice. One early Christian handbook advised that Christians should be baptized in running water (*Didache* 7.1–2).

After the baptism, early Christians would undergo a chrismation, an anointing with oil. This was not a direct requirement in the New Testament, but the practice was derived from New Testament themes, based on the language of anointing in texts like 2 Corinthians 1:21—"it is God who

---

[4] For more on this biblical theme and its use in patristic theology, see my previous work on the subject: Burden, *Who We Were Meant to Be*, 7–48.

establishes us with you in Christ, and has anointed us"—and 1 John 2:27—"the anointing that you received from him abides in you." Chrismation was the ritual that symbolized the receiving of the Holy Spirit (see Eph 1:13). The early apologist Tertullian connects the practice of chrismation directly with priestly ordination: "After that, we come up from the washing and are anointed with the blessed unction, following that ancient practice by which, ever since Aaron was anointed by Moses, there was a custom of anointing them for priesthood with oil" (*On Baptism* 7).

The third part of a priestly initiation was the robing, also a part of the baptismal rite. After coming up out of the water, the baptizand would receive a white garment. This garment hearkens back to the priest's linen tunic, the piece worn by the high priest when entering the Holy of Holies. A Christian undergoing baptism would have come away with the impression that they were being ordained to a priestly office.

But what does it mean to say that Christians are priests? Nowadays, most Christians—if they think of the idea of a Christian's priesthood at all—probably envision it in terms of *access*. To be a priest, we believe, means that we have immediate access to the presence of the Father through the mediation of Christ. Whereas in the Old Testament the common people were not allowed to enter within the central building of the temple, the priests could. So for us to be priests must mean that we can now draw near to God without needing any human intermediary besides Jesus.

Such an interpretation of the believer's priesthood is applicable and proper. It draws on biblical themes about the believer's position in Christ, and so it certainly has a place in the discussion. It is not, however, what the biblical passages about royal priesthood appear to be addressing. We tend to focus on the rights and privileges that being a priest would entail, but other cultures tended to look first to duties. To early Christian ears, saying that Christians share in an office of royal priesthood would imply a set of duties to be performed: worship and prayer supreme among them. As royal officers of God's kingdom and priests of his New-Creation-temple in Christ, we have a job to do, just like the priests of the Old Testament did.

> *As royal officers of God's kingdom and priests of his New-Creation-temple in Christ, we have a job to do.*

This is exactly what the New Testament passages which touch on royal priesthood do: they speak immediately of duties, not of privileges or rights. In both 1 Peter and Revelation, the immediate application of the royal priesthood imagery is the practical duties that we ought to undertake. First Peter 2:9 says that as God's royal priesthood, we are called to declare his praises. Revelation 5:10 says that we are appointed to serve. The answer is given in terms of duties, not access, despite how applicable the latter answer might be.

Priestly Duties

How were these duties understood? First and foremost, they were understood in the context of the weekly worship gathering. If the priests of the Old Testament were mainly responsible for offering sacrifices on the altar, early Christians thought that their whole worship service was offered to God as a sacrifice. As Psalm 50 clearly stated, God was seeking worshipers who would offer thanksgiving as their sacrifice to him (vv. 14, 23). The author of Hebrews picked up on this theme, describing Christian worship as a "sacrifice of praise" (Heb 13:15). The New Testament also speaks about our giving, good deeds, and life of faith in the context of sacrifice (Phil 2:17; 4:18; Heb 13:16; Rom 12:1). Sacrifice—a priestly duty—was seen as the center of Christian life and worship.

Two texts, Psalm 57:9 and Malachi 1:11, were held as being of primary importance in understanding the place of Christian worship in God's plan for the world.

> I will give thanks to you, O Lord, among the peoples;
> I will sing praises to you among the nations.—Psalm 57:9

> For from the rising of the sun to its setting my name will be great among the nations, and in every place incense will be offered to my name,
> and a pure offering. For my name will be great among the nations, says the LORD of hosts.—Malachi 1:11

Here we see a direct link between worship and the global extent of God's kingdom. These two passages shaped early Christianity's sense of mission—and of worship's place at the heart of mission—even more than Christ's Great Commission did. Psalm 57:9 and Malachi 1:11 were taken as prophecies which the church fulfilled every time it met for worship. For example, the *Didache* directly references Malachi 1:11 when discussing the Christian worship service (14.1–3). In the Malachi passage, the worship of the nations is described in the language of priestly tasks. Christians saw themselves as the fulfillment of that description, offering incense, prayer, praise, and thanksgiving to God as his royal priesthood. The east Syrian father Ephrem referred to the church as the mystery of God's plan, "to which were to come the vows and sacrifices of all the nations."[5] This sensibility about worship is reflected in the name which tradition gave to it: liturgy (*leitourgia*), "the work of the people." Worship is the high and necessary work of bearing pure sacrifices of praise and thanksgiving into the presence of God.

This perspective is not just an interpretation from the age of the early church fathers; it is rooted in the New Testament itself. When Romans 12:1 says that the offering of our bodies is our "true and proper worship" (NIV) or "spiritual worship" (ESV), Paul uses a phrase which carries a distinct connotation of *service* (the direct translation is "reasonable service"). In other words, Paul places us in a ministry of serving, a role of offering worship up to God. Worship was not conceived as something purely spiritual; it was a practical thing, the fulfillment of a necessary and important function. It is no accident that in the English tradition, we have come to call it a "service," for this is when we serve.

Justin Martyr, the second-century apologist, puts it succinctly: "We are now of the true priestly family of God, as he himself testifies when he says that in every place among the Gentiles pure and pleasing sacrifices are offered up to him [Mal 1:11]. But God receives sacrifices from no one, except through his priests." Justin goes on to list prayers, thanksgivings, and communion as some of the forms of Christian sacrifice (*Dialogue with Trypho* 116–17). Other church fathers also tie the themes of Christian identity and priestly service together. John Chrysostom refers to giving alms, praying for others, and living a life of virtue as the sacrifices "whereof each one is himself the priest" (*Homilies on Hebrews* 11.5–7). Cyril of Jerusalem says that the weekly worship service is "the spiritual sacrifice, the worship without blood" (*Mystagogic Catecheses* 5.8). Tertullian mentions the prayers of the worship service in these familiar terms of sacrifice: "We are … the true priests who, praying in spirit, sacrifice in spirit: prayer, a [sacrifice] proper and acceptable to God" (*On Prayer* 28).

Serving in Prayer and Holiness

Prayer was not simply one aspect of the worship service; the whole service of worship was considered an expression of prayer. All the songs, litanies, responses, and chants were directed to God. The early Christian service of worship was so saturated in prayer that the early church father Ignatius could describe it simply as "Eucharist and prayer" (*To the Smyrnaeans* 6.2). In the book of Acts, every gathering of the apostolic community in Jerusalem was suffused with prayer (1:14; 2:42; 3:1; 4:24–31; 6:4; 12:12). One of the main themes of the prayers in early Christian services was requests for mercy

---

5 Quoted in Murray, *Symbols of Church and Kingdom*, 45.

(based in part on the publican's cry recorded in Luke 18:13—"God, have mercy on me, a sinner"); another was thanksgiving. Long litanies of praise and thanksgiving wove throughout the service of worship, thus providing a real and practical fulfillment of the vision of Psalm 50—worshipers who bring to God a sacrifice of thanksgiving.

There's another interesting feature of early Christian prayers. They can be profoundly broad in their scope and wildly optimistic in their requests. This tendency appears nowhere more clearly than in their prayers for the nations. Early Christians were not afraid to pray big prayers. Justin Martyr reports that Christians pray for "all people everywhere" (*First Apology* 65). Other church fathers show similar patterns in prayer: Clement of Rome asks God to pour out grace upon all Christians throughout the world (*1 Clement* 59.2); Ignatius prays for all humanity, including our own enemies (*To the Ephesians* 10.1; *To the Smyrnaeans* 4.1); and Polycarp prays for all the nations (*To the Philippians* 12.3).

There's an example of this tendency from the life of Polycarp, a member of the apostolic fathers (the post-apostle generation of Christian leaders). When he was eighty-six years old, the Roman magistrate in Smyrna called for his arrest. Polycarp fled the city and found refuge in a cottage in the hills. But the Roman officers found him anyway, and Polycarp welcomed his pursuers and invited them to a meal in the cottage. When they had finished the meal, he asked if he could pray before they took him away. They agreed, so Polycarp stood up and prayed out loud for two hours, astonishing the officers with the grace, joy, and godliness of his prayer, in which he interceded for "everyone who had ever come into contact with him, both small and great, known and unknown, and all the universal church throughout the world" (*Martyrdom of Polycarp* 7.1–8.1).

> *The worship of the local church was not only one of the great goals of world mission, it was also the facilitator of that mission.*

These prayers, so broad in their scope, were so common that they became part of a cycle of liturgies used all across the Christian world. The worship of the local church was not only one of the great goals of world mission, it was also the facilitator of that mission. Prayer, as one of the Christian's highest priestly duties, called the believer to represent the whole world before the throne of God.

Not just prayer, but holiness too is part of our great priestly calling. Early Christianity's conviction about the importance of holiness helps make sense of the central role which ascetic and monastic models held in the church's mission. Personal holiness was not considered as something separate from the march of Christ's reign across the world; rather, it was the first and foremost battlefield in that advance. The same imagery of conquest and reign that motivated certain aspects of early Christian mission also motivated the ascetic labors of its missionary-monks.

Patristic writers conceived of the call to holiness not only as part of our priestly identity, but as part of our royal identity too. We were created from the beginning as rulers of creation, commissioned to have dominion, to fill the earth and subdue it (Gen 1:26, 28). According to the creation accounts, we were made from the dust of the earth, so our call to subdue the earth begins by subduing the earth represented in our own beings—our own rebellious hearts. God's mission for human beings—to exercise the dominion of administering his reign upon the earth—begins in us. Christians must rule their unruly hearts, constantly learning to submit to the reign of Christ, and in so doing we take the first steps in fulfilling our original commission of subduing the earth.

The church father Basil directly connects the idea of our ruling commission to the call for personal holiness: "O human, you are a ruling being. And why do you serve the passions as a slave? Why do you throw away your own dignity and become a slave of sin? … You were appointed ruler of creation, and you have renounced the nobility of your own nature" (*On the Origin of Humanity*, Discourse 1.8). Our call to exercise and administer the reign of God begins with us. Reinstated to our original office through the reign of the new Adam, we exercise our royal powers by planting the flag of his kingdom in the battlefield of our own hearts.

Early Christians, following Paul's teaching in 1 Corinthians 15, saw their own period of history as the active reign of Christ, who is engaged in the work of putting all his enemies under his feet (1 Cor 15:25). His defeat of sin can be claimed and realized in our own lives as we conform ourselves ever more in submission to his reign. In this view, the pursuit of personal holiness is not in a different category of Christian activity than mission is; both are expressions of the advance of Christ's reign. Holiness is not just a quality that makes the missionary more effective; it is part of the mission itself.

> *Holiness is not just a quality that makes the missionary more effective; it is part of the mission itself.*

By marshaling our efforts and striving against the hold of sin in our lives, we participate in the ongoing march of Christ against his enemies. This battlefield imagery was very much at home with the way early Christians wrote and spoke. Consider Tertullian's encouragement to imprisoned Christians, reminding them that they were "called to the warfare of the living God" (*To the Martyrs* 3). Some eastern Christian groups, like the Sons and Daughters of the Covenant, conceived of baptism as a rite of enrollment in the army of Christ, in which Christians take up arms against demonic powers and their own sins.

One of these images used in early Christian texts to describe the process of growing in holiness was that of the arena. Christians are called to enter the arena of our own hearts, to subdue the wild beasts of our fallen sinful nature, and so to bring our own little battlefield into submission to the reign of Christ. Clement of Rome, admonishing his readers against jealousy, says, "We write these things, dear friends, not only to admonish you but also to remind ourselves. For we are in the same arena, and the same contest awaits us" (*1 Clement* 7.1). The patristic Bible scholar Jerome uses arena imagery too: "It is for you to choose whether you will enter the arena and win the crown" (*Letter* 130). The quest for personal holiness was seen as the frontline battlefield of God's mission in the world. As such, it should come as no surprise that the motivations which drove missionaries are often tied up with their own pursuit of a holy life.

The Imitation of Christ

As we have seen throughout the story of early Christianity, missionary motivations were seldom limited to a single aspect like compassion or obedience to Scripture. Rather, missionary motivations grew out of a complex theological worldview. Early Christian expansion was driven by a conviction of the reality of Christ's reign and the centrality of the worshiping community as its chief expression. Mission arose naturally from these convictions, but mission wasn't so much a goal in and of itself, as it was a result of Christianity's pursuit of that grander picture of the church's response to the reign of Christ. To have churches in all places, continually raising a sacrifice of praise and thanksgiving before the king in fulfillment of Malachi 1:11—that was the vision that framed the goals of early Christian mission.

In addition to that broad, communally oriented view of Christian expansion, much missionary activity was driven by a desire to pursue a holistically Christian mode of life. Men and women from across the Christian world sought ways to imitate the life of Christ more closely or to devote all their attention to prayer and contemplation. These desires for an all-encompassing holiness, taken to the fullest measure of daily practice, drove the development of several different types of monasticism. While it might seem at first that monks living in utter seclusion would not be the most effective agents of mission, the historical record reveals that they were almost always on the forefront of Christian expansion.

Even the monks who sought to live in the utmost seclusion from any human society eventually found that they could not hide away completely. Simeon Stylites, famous for secluding himself on the top of a pillar in the desert for most of his life, drew large crowds from the surrounding hinterlands to hear him speak and to request his prayers. Antony, the towering early figure of Egyptian monasticism, became so famous for his asceticism that he had to retreat further and further into the wilderness just to get away from the people who came out to see him. This perpetual movement to the margins led hermit-style monks, particularly in places like eastern Syria and Palestine, into contact with new people groups across cultural and linguistic boundaries. Like the people of the empire, these new groups were drawn to the strange, holy men and came to them requesting prayer and counsel.

In other places, forms of monasticism developed that were profoundly missional in every respect. This was the case with the two most prominent missionary movements in early Christianity: east Syria/the Church of the East on one hand, and the Celtic/Anglo-Saxon mission movement on the other. The individual forms of what it meant to be a monk varied, but in both cases they were modeled on the idea of wandering rather than simple seclusion. East Syrian missionaries, following the example of Addai, took Jesus's mission instructions in Luke 10 as their model, wandering about in pairs and living the life of the kingdom. "The motivation for ascetic monasticism," writes Christoph Baumer, "lay in the ideal of the imitation of Christ."[6] In the Celtic model, this approach to the monastic life was considered a type of martyrdom, a resignation of the stability and security of normal life in order to live like Jesus and his disciples had lived. It was an attempt to conform one's practice as close as possible to the way Jesus lived in the gospels.

This tendency was not the spontaneous creation of Persia or Ireland; it was rooted in the earliest generations of Christian faith. Converts in the first few centuries, says historian Judith Herrin, were marked by an almost quasi-monastic fervor to adopt a lifestyle like that of Jesus and the apostles:

> In homes, whole families adopted a style of life modelled on that of the Apostles; some devoted themselves to missionary work, others to charitable deeds among the outcasts of Roman society .... Some took vows of chastity and seclusion, dedicating themselves to prayer in what were in effect house monasteries. Still others left their homes completely and sought to escape the temptations of the world.[7]

---

6 Baumer, *Church of the East*, 126.
7 Herrin, *Formation of Christendom*, 57.

The imitation of Christ, as an all-encompassing manner of life, was a theme that arose over and over again throughout early and medieval Christianity, and its direct result was the expanding geographical reach of the gospel.

Once again, as in the case of the early church's emphasis on the reign of Christ, we see mission arising as a consequence of a larger theological vision, but not necessarily as a primary goal in and of itself. Most of the wandering monks were not setting out with the express aim to be missionaries (though a few were); most were simply setting out to be like Jesus, with the expectation that God would use that lifestyle to further the work of his kingdom. The overriding importance of personal holiness as a means of doing mission thus appears once again.

> *Most were simply setting out to be like Jesus, with the expectation that God would use that lifestyle to further the work of his kingdom.*

Chapter 9

Mission in the Spirit of Early Christianity

When we begin to study the missionary enterprise of early Christianity, we are immediately confronted by the fact that it does not always resemble mission as we might know it. Though we know that Christianity grew rapidly in the Roman Empire over the first few centuries, we have only a few hints as to how it grew, and still less to what motivated Christians to evangelism or mission. References to evangelistic preaching after the apostolic period are few and far between, and we have only a handful of recorded instances of person-to-person evangelistic witnessing. Rather, we find that the means of evangelism which received the greatest emphasis within the Roman Empire were martyrdoms, exorcisms, healings, and the like. While we should not discount the presence of individual witnessing and other, more passive forms of evangelism (like the display of charity and the attractive moral sense of Christianity), it is noteworthy that the missionary methods highlighted by early Christian writers are somewhat different than what later generations of Christians might expect.

> *Early Christian expansion appears to have been motivated less by Jesus's commands and more by his pattern of life.*

When we pry a little deeper and attempt to reconstruct the early Christian perception of the missionary mandate—in other words, what motivated them to missionary activity—we find still more differences. Many of the most commonly articulated motivations in our day appear only sparsely in early records, if at all. Concern for the spiritual state of others does not appear to have been a driving motive (except in times and places where a sense of kinship drove that concern, as with the expansion of Arian Christianity among the Goths or the Anglo-Saxon missions to Frisia). Obedience to biblical commands also only appears rarely, and almost never with the Great

Commission in view. Rather, early Christian expansion appears to have been motivated less by Jesus's commands and more by his pattern of life, along with the inspiring vision of Old Testament prophecy, which Christians believed they were fulfilling.

There are two extreme responses to this discrepancy between early Christianity's motivations and those of our own day. The first is to accept wholeheartedly the early Church's understandings and methods simply because they were nearer to the fountainhead of our faith than we are. The other extreme is to utterly disregard the work of the early church and to assume that the Holy Spirit took an extended vacation until the Protestant Reformation. Neither of these reactions is acceptable.

Against the first position, we would say that the earliness of the early church is not in itself a convincing argument for the authority of their faith and practice. It may be the case that they retained certain themes and emphases of the apostles' preaching that were not ultimately included in the canon of Scripture, and that is worthy of consideration. However, Christianity has long believed that the witness of Scripture contains what is necessary for proper belief, so any Christian tradition which is rooted in Scripture can feel itself on solid ground. What the early church does offer us, however, is the possibility that our *interpretation* of Scripture may have gotten off track at some point, and that their perceptions of the meaning of certain passages may be closer to the truth than our own. Sometimes the presuppositions of our culture blind us to certain facets of Scripture, just as the culture of the Roman Empire did for the early church—but their blindnesses will not be the same as ours, so we can expect that the records they left behind may help us to perceive the weak spots in our own understanding.

Against the second position, there is almost no concrete historical evidence to which one can point to make the argument that the entirety of early Christianity fell immediately into pervasive error. To ignore the history of the early and medieval church is to turn our backs on a thousand years of the Holy Spirit's ministry in the world. However, the church is also an institution made up of humans, and therefore fallible in a number of ways. Though the Holy Spirit is working in the church, Christians don't always get everything right as a result. Therefore, as we would do with the varying expressions of Christian faith in our own time, we must use a discerning eye towards the early and medieval churches, seeking to separate the wheat from the chaff. This is no easy task, since our assumptions often lead us to favor our own position where we disagree with our spiritual forebears. Along the way, though, we may find something of value, something that we in our ignorance have overlooked or forgotten.

With that in mind, the following areas for reflection and application emerge from the witness of early Christianity's missionary motivations.

A Christus Victor Missiology

One of the dominant conceptions of early Christianity's soteriology (that is, its theology of salvation) was represented by the paradigm known as Christus Victor. In short, Christus Victor theology considers the work of Christ not just as an act of sacrificial atonement that leads to the forgiveness of sins, but as the triumph of God over the powers of sin, death, and the devil.

In this view, our problem, in our natural condition without Christ, is that we are captives. Everyone who sins cedes power to Satan and his dominion over the earth. There is a broad stream of Scripture that speaks about Satan's present dominion over the world, and about the Christian life as an external battle against the powers of evil. Paul refers to Satan as "the god of this world" (2 Cor 4:4) and "the prince of the power of the air" (Eph 2:2). Jesus calls Satan "the prince" of this present age (John 12:31; 14:30; 16:11). Further, the early church fathers saw death as more than just a physical eventuality—it was an evil spiritual power, now wielded by Satan, to which all human beings were subject as a result of sin. It included not merely physical death, but the loss of all spiritual life. To these three complementary spheres of evil power—Satan, sin, and death—all human beings were enslaved as a result of Adam and Eve's first sin and our own subsequent rebellion against God's ways.

In this view, the life, death, resurrection, and ascension of Jesus all have significance for our salvation (rather than an overriding focus on his death alone, which other views of atonement tend to highlight). The gospels are full of Jesus's confrontation with the powers of evil. He prepared for his ministry by going into the desert and ended up having a faceoff with Satan. A large part of Jesus's subsequent ministry consisted of the confrontation of demonic powers and freeing people from their grasp. Finally, Jesus died on the cross "that through death he might destroy the one who has the power of death, that is, the devil, and deliver all those who through fear of death were subject to lifelong slavery" (Heb 2:14–15; cf. Col 2:15; 1 John 3:8). As the final stroke of his victory, Jesus rose from the dead. The power of death, which was in Satan's hands, could not hold him. Rising in triumph, he then ascended to reign. Like the vision of Daniel 7:13–14, the Son of Man ascended through the clouds, up to the throne of the Ancient of Days, and was granted a dominion that manifests itself in the worship of all peoples and nations.

Soteriology tends to undergird missionary methods and motivations, so it is no surprise that a culture with Christus Victor theology as a primary lens appears to function on a different missiological wavelength than later

Protestant groups, many of whom have had a view of substitutionary atonement as their primary soteriological lens. In early Christianity, the view of mission envisioned a triumphal war against Satan and the powers of evil, and so Christians employed spiritual warfare as the frontline tactics of its mission. Exorcisms, healings, and displays of supernatural power went side-by-side with the gospel message. Not only was the salvation of individuals a wonderful thing for the individuals themselves, it was a blow against the enemy, whose kingdom of darkness was shrinking with every new convert that was transferred into the kingdom of light.

The ancient baptismal liturgies usually included a renunciation of Satan (sometimes including physical actions, like turning away from Satan or symbolically spitting on him). When such a convert was asked to renounce Satan, the early church was not speaking of personal spirituality and individual sin. It was a declaration of war—a renunciation of the old king and an acceptance of the colors of the *Militia Christi*. In the eastern Christianity of Mesopotamia, vast throngs of people consecrated themselves as "Sons and Daughters of the Covenant," pledged to do spiritual battle through preaching, healing, charity, and prayer. And when the desert fathers in Egypt withdrew to the wilderness to give themselves to a life of prayer, it wasn't simply for the sake of eccentricity or austere personal devotion—it was to confront the demons head-on in the desert wastelands and in the battlefields of their own hearts. The mission of the church was not so much concerned with reaching unreached people as it was with making Christ's triumph over Satan an experienced reality in the world around them.

> *In early Christianity, the view of mission envisioned a triumphal war against Satan and the powers of evil.*

So what can the early church suggest for our present theology of missions? It would be unwise to abandon the clearly biblical passion for the salvation of individuals, but that doesn't mean that we can't buttress it with the addition of a Christus Victor perspective. The two views are complementary and produce a stronger theological framework when held together than when only one is held. Consider, for instance, one of the drawbacks of holding a missiology that focuses exclusively on the salvation of souls: if a missionary enterprise does not ultimately gain any converts, it can be regarded as a profound disappointment. The history of modern mission movements is replete with examples of missionary labors carried out in very difficult environments for making converts—places in which other religions or philosophies maintain a rigid hold on people's lives. The slow progress of Christian mission in such places can at times feel disheartening to those who are engaged in it.

If we add a Christus Victor element, however, the picture changes. In this light, missionary work in the most difficult places is the most important, the most daring, and possibly the most fruitful work of all, since it stands on the front lines of the great spiritual war. Missionaries in those places are claiming the first beachhead in hostile territory, and simply by being there and manifesting the life of the kingdom in that place, they weaken the power of the enemy's usurped dominions. In Christus Victor theology, no missionary endeavor carried out in the spirit of Christ can be a failure, simply because every such effort, regardless of the visible results, is a blow against Satan's kingdom. Obedience to the call of Christ is never in vain. Any effort that says "yes" to God's mission in the world is inherently valuable. Christus Victor theology reminds us that it is Christ who is the warrior, and Christ who is the victor—not us. Our part is to obey; his part is to bring forth whatever fruit may grow, whether the field looks fruitful or barren.

> *In Christus Victor theology, no missionary endeavor carried out in the spirit of Christ can be a failure.*

Optimism Grounded in the Reality of Christ's Reign

One of the most impressive features of Christianity's rise was its optimism. Even in the earliest period, when Christians were still a despised and persecuted minority, their writings reveal a wild sense of confidence that their faith would be the eventual destiny of the entire world. They expected that the entire world would prove to be the scope of the Messiah's reign, not only in the age to come, but in the present period of world history. The patristic Bible scholar Origen wrote, "Every form of worship will be destroyed except the religion of Christ, which alone will prevail. Indeed, it will one day triumph" (*Against Celsus* 8.68). Gerald Sittser sums up this early Christian attitude well: "It was bound to happen because Christianity is true. ... In Jesus truth triumphed, once and for all."[1]

Early Christians believed they saw signs of the prophecies of the messianic age coming true all around them. While most patristic writers taught that the culmination of Christ's reign would not appear until his second coming, their work reflected the idea that the messianic reign had already begun and that its effects could be seen on every side.

In the apologist Justin Martyr's dialogue with a Jewish man, Trypho, he tackles Trypho's objection that Jesus was last seen publicly when he died on a cross like a common criminal, which was a far cry from the expectations of

---

1 Sittser, *Resilient Faith*, 51.

glory, enthronement, and reign that the prophecies might lead one to expect of the Messiah (*Dialogue with Trypho* 32, 36, 39). Justin responds by arguing that the messianic kingdom has obviously begun to arise through Jesus, because the prophecies about it were in the process of being fulfilled in visible and demonstrable ways. "If all nations are blessed in the Messiah [Ps 72:17], and we who are from all nations believe in him, then he is the Messiah, and we are they who are blessed through him" (121; cf.109–10). Essentially, Justin's argument is that Jesus has accomplished one of the defining features of the prophesied messianic age: the nations of the world are coming to worship the God of Israel. As Athanasius also notes, "The whole earth is filled with the knowledge of God, and the Gentiles … are now taking refuge in the God of Abraham through the Word, even our Lord Jesus Christ" (*On the Incarnation* 40). To the Christian, this was proof that the messianic reign had begun.

This optimistic triumphalism was firmly rooted in Old Testament prophecy. Central to their understanding of Jesus's messianic identity were texts like Psalm 2, which speaks to the king and identifies him as Christ ("anointed") and as the son of God (vv. 2, 6–7, 12). Further, the text says to him, "I will make the nations your heritage, and the ends of the earth your possession" (v. 8). Another central messianic text was Psalm 110, which speaks to someone identified as "lord" and as a priest in the order of Melchizedek (vv. 1, 4), and portrays this person's reign as being a triumph over his enemies: "Sit at my right hand, until I make your enemies your footstool" (v. 1). Early Christians tended to take these prophecies to heart, basing their view of the world on them. Even though there would still clearly be new areas to be reached with the gospel, they viewed the spread of Christ's reign as a given, almost as something already accomplished. "The whole world," says Clement of Alexandria, "has already become the domain of the Word" (*Exhortation to the Heathen* 11). Tertullian says the same: "Christ's name is extending everywhere, believed everywhere … reigning everywhere, adored everywhere" (*An Answer to the Jews* 7).

One of the most common arguments of early Christian apologetics was simply to point out that the pagan cults appeared completely unable to stop their rise. In fact, one of the reasons that early monastics went out into the wilderness to pray was because they felt that the gospel had already triumphed over the pagan cults in the cities, and so they were chasing the demons out of their last strongholds in the desert. These hermits were not just seeking a life of seclusion from the world. Rather, they conceived of their work as spiritual warfare, in which they continued to push back the powers of Satan, in the battlefield of their own souls and in the desert wastes.

Mission in the Spirit of Early Christianity

The victory of Christ and the manifestation of his reign emerge as the driving theological forces behind early Christian mission. One of the most common themes in early Christian artwork was an abbreviation that was written alongside images of Jesus: *IC XC NIKA*, "Jesus Christ conquers." This "conquering" did not carry overtones of military advance, colonialism, or imperialism; it was an expression of Jesus's victory over the powers of evil in the spiritual realm and the ongoing progress of his reign (Col 2:15; 1 Cor 15:25). If understood correctly, a Christus Victor missiology would never lead to imperialism. In the Christus Victor view, the enemy is always a spiritual enemy—Satan and the spiritual powers that undergird systems of oppression. The enemy is never another human being, not even if they are acting in the guise of an enemy toward us. Rather, those people are the very ones in need of the deliverance from captivity, a deliverance only available by coming under the reign of Christ.

Mission, when undertaken in the spirit of early Christianity, ought to display a sense of patient confidence. The incredible global spread of the gospel of Jesus Christ has already demonstrated that it stands in the center of the fulfillment of Old Testament prophecies. The nations are coming together to worship the God of Israel, just as the prophets had said. With that confirmation in place, we can have every confidence, even in the face of setbacks and persecutions, that God will prove true to his word, and that the reigning King will put all his enemies under his feet.

> *Mission, when undertaken in the spirit of early Christianity, ought to display a sense of patient confidence.*

Mission and the Church

One of the other applications from early Christian mission is the centrality they placed upon planting worshiping communities. The development of a church or monastic group was the main goal, for which conversions were a contributing factor, but the life of the church held center stage. As we saw in chapter 7, this tendency is rooted in their understanding of the reign of Christ, the fulfilment of Old Testament prophecies, and the sacramental meaning of Christian worship within God's plan for the world.

The presence of a church—even if only composed of the mission team members itself—was thought to be a tremendously significant thing in the mind of early Christianity. It was a partial realization of the prophecy of Malachi 1:11, as pure offerings of praise and thanksgiving are raised before the throne of God from every place on earth. Further, early Christians believed that the weekly worship of the church was the central act of our duty as God's royal priesthood. Engaged in prayer together, Christians were part of God's work of bringing all things together under Christ (Eph 1:10), serving as a living bridge of union between heaven and earth. The worship of the church was a mystical event which served as an eschatological sign of the fullness of Christ's kingdom, a connection point between time and eternity. It was also a practical and visible embassy of Christ's reign, existing in the midst of earthly dominions.

One of the aspects of the ministry of reconciliation which was incarnated in the church was the binding together of different people groups. The clearest sign of God's work in bringing all things back together was the union of disparate cultures, ethnicities, and languages within the worshiping communities of the church. In the unity of the church, the prophecies of the Old Testament began to have their realization. The curse of Babel, in which the families of the world were torn apart, was now being reversed in the church, as those families came back together in the harmony of the service of God. Mission can properly count reconciliation ministries as part of its essential calling, striving to bring together the peoples of the world into a united identity as the people of God.

To do mission in the spirit of early Christianity, the establishment of worshiping communities should be in the forefront, not only because of what churches can *do*, but simply because what churches *are*. The temptation in our utilitarian culture is to think about churches in terms of their practical value—as bases from which further outreach can be launched, and as necessary hubs for furthering discipleship among Christians. Early Christianity would bid us to think highly of the place of churches because of what they represent. They are symbols and signs of the kingdom, offering services which bind heaven and earth together in the work of God and the fulfillment of Scripture. Early Christian mission was mission with a high ecclesiology.

Christian Mission in Hostile Cultures

The shape of early Christian mission can also inform our approach to hostile cultures (including, increasingly, a Western culture ever more skeptical of Christian claims). For its first three centuries, Christianity was a despised and persecuted minority within the Roman Empire. In other areas, like Persia, the period of facing a hostile and intolerant society stretched even longer.

Christianity's broad response to these cultural hostilities ran along two main lines. First, Christians simply sought to live good and holy lives, as encouraged to do in the New Testament epistles. By the patient grace of living day by day in the midst of non-Christian neighbors, exemplifying the love and peace of the gospel, Christians gradually came to be regarded more and more favorably by the people of the empire.

There is a temptation to try to dream up grand programs and strategies for outreach, and to put our hope in those measures. While programs and strategies certainly have a place, the witness of both Scripture and history would bid us not to underestimate the powerful place of passive evangelism. The kingdom grows like yeast in a lump of dough, silently and slowly, but producing dramatic changes in the end. Again, as we have already observed, the primary way of spreading Christianity is, quite simply, to live it.

> *The primary way of spreading Christianity is, quite simply, to live it.*

Second, Christians were active in apologetics, particularly during the second and third centuries in the Roman Empire. Writers like Justin Martyr and Tertullian laid out measured, studious, well-reasoned arguments for the Christian faith in response to their critics. Popular criticisms of Christianity commonly ran into rumors and conspiracy theories, accusing Christians of being cannibals (for their practice of communion) and "atheists" who endangered pagan cities by not making sacrifices to the capricious local gods. Christians did not attempt to match this hysteria or to hit back with vicious polemics of their own; they simply stated their case in a way that comes across as confident, composed, and winsome. There is a call for this kind of apologetics in today's culture—one that does not allow itself to get dragged into the mud of bitterness or polemics, but which focuses on speaking the beauty of God's truth with grace and goodwill.

Another application arises largely out of the unconscious circumstances of early Christianity—that of being clearly and obviously a distinct people, set apart from the world. In their earliest days they were an odd and easily recognizable sect, and while this distinctiveness could attract persecution, it also sometimes played to their advantage. There was a sense of mystery about the church because it was so different from the rest of the world. It is worth asking whether that same sense of wonderful mystery surrounds the church in our contemporary contexts.

There's a famous story from the first millennium of Christian expansion which speaks to this theme, though it falls somewhat later than this book's main historical focus. It concerns the conversion of Kievan Rus to the Christian faith, an account which has gone down in legend. Vladimir, the reigning prince of Kiev, considered all the various religious options around him (Islam, Judaism, Roman Catholicism, and Eastern Orthodoxy), and he chose Eastern Orthodox Christianity because it was so beautiful. His emissaries returned from their visit to Constantinople's Hagia Sophia church with their account of being so struck with wonder that they did not know if they were in heaven or on earth. Christians would do well to consider how to present Christianity's beauty within the cultures we address.

The early medieval church also gives us an intriguing institutional paradigm to consider: missional monasticism. Protestants have long tended to shy away from monasticism. There is a common stereotype, not wholly undeserved, that the secluded lifestyle of monks ignores the Christian mandate of outreach, of being "in the world but not of it." However, the early Celtic monasticism of Columba and Columbanus presents a rather different picture. Instead of being communities of seclusion, these monasteries were communities of outreach. The monks lived together in poverty and under mutual spiritual vows, but they also went out into the surrounding areas, teaching and preaching to the local residents. Eventually a new monastery would be planted on the frontiers of an unreached territory, and the monks would go about preaching and teaching there as well, until a new set of missionary-monks were trained and ready to go even further into the barbarian hinterland.

Monasticism is a peculiar enough institution that it will likely not be missionally effective in every cultural context, but it should at least be available as an option in the Christian toolkit for engaging with any given culture. If a group of Christians—either singly or in families—elected to live together in a common community, holding resources in common and strengthening one another's spiritual lives by their constant contact, all while going out into the world and intentionally living the witness of the gospel there, what would the effects be? It should be noted that this is not merely a historical model; it is also a biblical model, being very similar to the early Jerusalem church as portrayed in Acts.

Building a Missionary Culture

Another set of applications that we can take from the history of the early and medieval church is on the matter of how to build a missionary culture. There were two great instances of missionary cultures during this period—the east-Syrian model of the Church of the East and the Celtic/Anglo-Saxon missions. For Christian clerics in those cultures, missionary service was regarded as one of the highest ideals, one of the greatest honors of the life of faith. They sent out missionaries in all directions at a rate unsurpassed until the Jesuits and the Moravians of the post-Reformation world.

How were they able to motivate their people so readily for missionary service? There seem to have been two main reasons: first, the heroes of whom they were told while growing up were all missionaries; and second, the finest churchmen and scholars of the day were involved in missionary service. The legacy of Patrick and Columbanus, along with a host of seventh-century missionary-wanderers, fueled the Anglo-Saxon mission-wave that was spearheaded by Willibrord and Boniface. Their heroes were all missionaries, and so they too aspired to be missionaries. In the same way that ministry students in contemporary America might aspire to become like Billy Graham or Rick Warren, they aspired to become like Patrick, Columba, and Aidan. The church historian Bede continued this legacy with his mission-minded book, *Ecclesiastical History of the English People*, which became common reading in England and France and later served to spark the ninth-century missions of the Carolingian renaissance.

The second reason for these missionary cultures was that the finest minds of the day were involved in mission. Egbert, Willibrord, and Boniface represented the cream of the crop of Anglo-Saxon clerics, and rather than spend their lives gaining large followings in England, they decided to spend themselves on the mission field. A similar dynamic would play out later in history, when two of the brightest lights in the Byzantine Empire, Cyril and Methodius, forsook the glory awaiting them at home, and instead set out to bring the gospel to the Slavs of eastern Europe. If the visible leaders of church cultures make the public sacrifice of serving in cross-cultural mission for the sake of the kingdom, it has far-reaching effects in raising up admirers to join the cause.

Personal Holiness as Mission

Much of the early and medieval church also operated on a somewhat different conception of what the ideal Christian life should look like. While many modern Christians might point to a life characterized by daily times of devotion, personal witness in word and deed, and a healthy family life, some traditions in early Christianity pointed to something rather different, something that looked quite a bit like the pattern of ministry Jesus laid out for his followers in Luke 10. This was especially true in the eastern Christianity of Syria, Mesopotamia, and Persia from the second through the seventh centuries, and in Celtic and Anglo-Saxon Christianity from the sixth through the eighth centuries. Their ideal was of the wandering pilgrim, wholly consecrated to Christ in every facet of one's life. This was "the imitation of Christ" considered not merely as a path of spiritual devotion, but as a whole way of living in the world. These imitators of Christ—usually monks—were considered set apart from the world, and they patterned their lives after Christ's own: walking from village to village, preaching the gospel, praying, voluntarily accepting the poverty of not having a home, and doing acts of charity.

One of the interesting differences between modern Christianity and early Christianity is apparent here. Most modern Christians take Jesus's Great Commission passages as binding not only on his own disciples, but on all Christians throughout history. Early Christianity, by contrast, tended to view those passages as applying only to Jesus's disciples, but not necessarily setting a pattern for all future generations. When it comes to other passages, however, like Jesus's specific mission instructions to his followers during his Galilean ministry (in Luke 10 and elsewhere), modern Christians tend to limit their application to the disciples, while early Christians saw in them a continuing pattern for future practice. Each side discounts one passage's application to themselves and accepts a different passage; the irony is that these two periods of Christianity did it entirely backwards from one another. The point here is not to assess which passage more clearly applies to later generations of Christians, but simply to note the way that differences in biblical interpretation lead to significant differences in missiology.

> *Their ideal was of the wandering pilgrim, wholly consecrated to Christ in every facet of one's life.*

In any case, the passages adopted by early Christianity pointed them in the direction of an ascetical framework for the imitation of Christ. The ascetic rigors of many early Christians were thus not the result of an over-spiritualization that denied the body; rather, in many cases it was in direct obedience to Christ's instructions for self-renunciation and wandering while proclaiming the kingdom. It was just such pilgrim-preachers who carried the gospel all the way into Persia, and then to China and the steppes of central Asia in the first millennium, and it was just such pilgrim-preachers who set out from Britain to convert the tribes of Frisia and Germany to the faith. These wandering pilgrims constituted the most significant missionary force in the first thousand years of Christianity.

While evangelism was certainly a conscious part of their mission, the ultimate aim was broader: to be as Christlike as possible, not only in one's spirituality but in all the little facets of everyday life. Conformity to Christ was the great goal of the ideal Christian life, and it manifested itself in the desire to live like Jesus did, which necessarily included acts of intentional outreach along the way. Mission flowed from the grand ambition to know Jesus more and to be made like him, much as the apostle Paul expressed it in his letters.

If we are to do mission in the spirit of early Christianity, then holiness of life must be among our highest goals. While not everyone can live the life of an ascetic wanderer, all Christians can work to make their identity as representatives of the life of the kingdom their highest value. The first task of mission, upon beginning an outreach or going to a new place, is quite simply to live as a Christian in that place, exemplifying the life of the kingdom there. In so doing, our interior battle for holiness continues the advance of the kingdom in our own hearts, while also empowering its expansion in the society around us. And like the people of the wilderness who were drawn out to see the monks in their labors, people cannot help but be drawn by the winsome vision of a life of reckless, daring, holy love.

This conflux of ideas—holiness, the imitation of Christ, the meaning of worship, the centrality of the church, and so on—is all bound up in a grand theological vision of Christian identity in the in-breaking kingdom of God. It is a vision that reaches to the ends of the earth, but which grounds itself not in expectations for particular results but in the hopeful assurance that the King is on the throne. Adding the insights of the early Christian period to the wisdom of our own missiology will strengthen the whole and will ready the church for the day when the kingdom comes in all its fullness, and the earth will be full of the knowledge of the glory of the Lord.

> *Mission flowed from the grand ambition to know Jesus more and to be made like him.*

Bibliography

Arpee, Leon. *A History of Armenian Christianity*. New York: Armenian Missionary Association of America, 1946.

Baumer, Christoph. *The Church of the East: An Illustrated History of Assyrian Christianity*. London: I. B. Tauris, 2006.

Berkley, Jonathan. *The Formation of Islam: Religion and Society in the Near East, 600–1800*. Cambridge: Cambridge University Press, 2003.

Binns, John. "Introduction." In *Cyril of Scythopolis: The Lives of the Monks of Palestine*, iv–lii. Kalamazoo: Cistercian Publications, 1991.

Brown, Peter. "The Rise and Function of the Holy Man in Late Antiquity." *Journal of Roman Studies* 61 (1971): 80–101.

Brown, Peter. *The Rise of Western Christendom*. 2nd ed. Malden: Blackwell, 2003.

Brown, Peter. *The World of Late Antiquity, AD 150–750*. New York: W. W. Norton & Co., 1971.

Burden, Matthew. *Who We Were Meant to Be: Rediscovering Our Role as God's Royal Priesthood*. Eugene: Wipf & Stock, 2021.

Clément, Olivier. *The Roots of Christian Mysticism: Text and Commentary*. New York: New City Press, 1993.

Cusack, Carole M. *The Rise of Christianity in Northern Europe, 300–1000*. New York: Cassell, 1998.

Davies, Norman. *Vanished Kingdoms: The Rise and Fall of States and Nations*. New York: Viking, 2011.

Donner, Fred M. *Muhammad and the Believers: At the Origins of Islam*. Cambridge, MA: Belknap Press, 2010.

Duckett, Eleanor. *The Wandering Saints of the Early Middle Ages*. New York: Norton, 1959.

Dunn, James D. G. *Did the First Christians Worship Jesus? The New Testament Evidence*. Louisville: Westminster John Knox Press, 2010.

Engberg-Pedersen, Troels. "Setting the Scene: Stoicism and Platonism in the Transitional Period in Ancient Philosophy." In *Stoicism in Early Christianity*, edited by Tuomas Rasimus, Troels Engberg-Pedersen, and Ismo Dunderberg, 1–14. Grand Rapids: Baker Academic, 2010.

Farmer, D. H. "Notes." In Bede, *Ecclesiastical History of the English People*, 361–74. New York: Penguin, 1990.

Fletcher, Richard. *The Barbarian Conversion: From Paganism to Christianity*. New York: Henry Holt, 1997.

Glass, John. *The Mission of Saint Mungo*. London: Athena Press, 2007.

Green, Michael. *Evangelism in the Early Church*. Grand Rapids: Eerdmans, 1970.

Hall, Christopher A. *Worshiping with the Church Fathers.* Downers Grove: InterVarsity Press, 2009.

Hart, David Bentley. *The Story of Christianity: A History of 2000 Years of the Christian Faith.* New York: Quercus, 2009.

Heather, Peter. "The Crossing of the Danube and the Gothic Conversion." *Greek, Roman and Byzantine Studies* 27 (1986): 289–318.

Heather, Peter, and John Matthews, eds. *The Goths in the Fourth Century.* Liverpool: Liverpool University Press, 1991.

Herrin, Judith. *The Formation of Christendom.* Princeton: Princeton University Press, 1987.

Hillgarth, J. N., ed. *Christianity and Paganism, 350–750: The Conversion of Western Europe.* Philadelphia: University of Pennsylvania Press, 1969.

Hinson, E. Glenn. *The Evangelization of the Roman Empire: Identity and Adaptability.* Macon: Mercer University Press, 1981.

Holme, L. R. *The Extinction of the Christian Churches in North Africa.* New York: Burt Franklin, 1898.

Isichei, Elizabeth. *A History of Christianity in Africa: From Antiquity to the Present.* Grand Rapids: Eerdmans, 1995.

Jenkins, Philip. *The Lost History of Christianity: The Thousand-Year Golden Age of the Church in the Middle East, Africa, and Asia—and How It Died.* New York: HarperOne, 2008.

Kreider, Alan. *The Patient Ferment of the Early Church: The Improbable Rise of Christianity in the Roman Empire.* Grand Rapids: Baker Academic, 2016.

Lane Fox, Robin. *Pagans and Christians.* New York: Knopf, 1987.

Latourette, Kenneth Scott. *A History of the Expansion of Christianity, Vol. 1: The First Five Centuries.* New York: Harper & Brothers, 1937.

Longenecker, Richard N. *The Christology of Early Jewish Christianity.* London: SCM Press, 1970.

MacMullen, Ramsay. *Christianizing the Roman Empire (AD 100–400).* New Haven: Yale University Press, 1984.

Marnell, William H. *Light from the West: The Irish Mission and the Emergence of Modern Europe.* New York: Seabury, 1978.

Mathisen, Ralph W. "Barbarian Bishops and the Churches 'in barbaricis gentibus' during Late Antiquity." *Speculum* 72, no. 3 (1997): 664–97.

Meyendorff, John. *Imperial Unity and Christian Divisions: The Church 450–680 AD.* Crestwood: Saint Vladimir's Seminary Press, 1989.

Mitchell, Stephen. *A History of the Later Roman Empire, AD 284–641.* Malden: Blackwell Publishing, 2007.

Moffett, Samuel Hugh. *A History of Christianity in Asia, Vol. 1: Beginnings to 1500.* Maryknoll: Orbis, 2008.

Murray, Robert. *Symbols of Church and Kingdom: A Study in Early Syriac Tradition.* London: Cambridge University Press, 1975.

Neill, Stephen. *A History of Christianity in India: The Beginnings to AD 1707.* Cambridge: Cambridge University Press, 1984.

Potter, David S. *The Roman Empire at Bay, AD 180–395.* London: Routledge, 2004.

Schnabel, Eckhard J. *Early Christian Mission, Vol. 2: Paul and the Early Church.* Downers Grove: InterVarsity Press, 2004.

Sivan, Hagith. "Ulfila's Own Conversion." *Harvard Theological Review* 89, no. 4 (1996): 373–86.

Smither, Edward L. *Mission in the Early Church: Themes and Reflections.* Eugene: Cascade, 2014.

Soro, Mar Bawai. *The Church of the East: Apostolic and Orthodox.* San Jose: Adiabene Publications, 2007.

Spurgeon, Charles H. *Spurgeon at His Best.* Edited by Tom Carter. Grand Rapids: Baker, 1991.

Stancliffe, C. E. "From Town to Country: The Christianization of the Touraine, 370–600." In *The Church in Town and Countryside*, edited by Derek Baker, 43–59. Oxford: Basil Blackwell, 1979.

Stark, Rodney. *The Rise of Christianity.* San Francisco: HarperCollins, 1997.

Trimingham, J. S. *Christianity among the Arabs in Pre-Islamic Times.* London: Longman, 1979.

Vantini, Giovanni. *Christianity in the Sudan.* Bologna: EMI, 1981.

Vine, Aubrey R. *The Nestorian Churches.* New York: AMS Press, 1980.

Waterfield, Robin E. *Christians in Persia: Assyrians, Armenians, Roman Catholics and Protestants.* New York: Harper & Row, 1973.

Wells, Peter S. *Barbarians to Angels: The Dark Ages Reconsidered.* New York: W. W. Norton & Co., 2008.

Welsby, Derek A. *The Medieval Kingdoms of Nubia: Pagans, Christians and Muslims along the Middle Nile.* London: British Museum Press, 2002.

Wright, N. T. *How God Became King: The Forgotten Story of the Gospels.* New York: HarperOne, 2012.

Index

A

Addai 93, 110
Aggai 41, 93
Aidan 123
Alamans 69
Alcuin 85
Alopen 43
Alwa. *See* Nubia
Antony the Great 93, 110
apologetics 21, 22, 118, 121
apologists 22
Arian Christianity 85, 113
Arianism 63, 69
Arians 63
Armenia 35
ascetic
  life 43
  models 107
  monasticism 110
  rigors 124
  wandering 97
asceticism 110
Athanasius 96, 118
Augustine (missionary) 79
Augustine of Hippo 62
Avitus, Bishop 69, 70

B

Bardaisan 102
Basil 63, 108
Bede 78–80, 84, 123
bishops 89, 97, 98
Boniface 84, 86, 87, 123
Britain 78, 79, 95, 124

C

celibacy 41
Chalcedon, Council of 53
charity 113, 116, 124
China 43, 124
chorepiscopos 90
chrismation 104
Christus Victor 115–117, 119
Church of the East 42, 43, 93, 97, 110, 122
Clement of Alexandria 118
Clement of Rome 107, 109
Clotilde 69
Clovis 69, 70, 84
Columba 70, 93, 122, 123
Columbanus 70, 93, 122, 123
communities, monastic 90
compassion 109
concern (as a missionary motivation) 79, 85, 87, 113
Constantine 23, 24, 42, 62
Cyprian 90
Cyril and Methodius 123
Cyril of Jerusalem 106

D

Denmark 86
Didache 21

E

ecclesiology 120
Edessa 42
Egbert 84, 85, 123
Egypt 24, 25, 52, 53, 93, 94, 116
Ephrem 105
Ethelbert of Kent, King 79
Eusebius 23
Eutychus (missionary to the Goths) 62
evangelism, active 17, 20
evangelism, passive 17, 121
exorcism(s) 22, 23, 113, 116

F

Franks 68–70
Frisia 84–88, 113, 124
Frisians 84, 85

G

Gaul 62, 68, 70, 84, 87
Georgia 35
Germany 84, 86–88, 124
Gothic tribes 85
Goths 62, 113
Great Commission 87, 95, 105, 114, 124
Gregory the Great, Pope 79

H

healing(s) 22, 35, 93, 113, 116
Hewald the Black 84
Hewald the White 84
holiness 88, 93, 95, 107–109, 111, 124, 125
Huns 62, 84

I

Ignatius 106, 107
imitation of Christ 85, 88, 109, 123–125
India 21, 35, 43
Iona 95
Ireland 62, 70, 84, 85, 95, 110
Irenaeus 21, 22
Islam 121
Italy 62

J

Jerome 109
John Chrysostom 25, 106
Justin Martyr 20, 22, 106, 107, 117, 121

K

kingdom of God 92, 96, 101, 102, 105, 125

L

Lindisfarne 95
Lull, Raymond (missionary bishop) 87

M

Makuria. *See* Nubia
martyrdom 84, 88, 97, 110, 113
martyr(s) 18, 84, 87
Mesopotamia 35, 88, 93, 116, 123
messianic age 117, 118
Minucius Felix 20, 22
miracles 22, 23, 35, 93
missionaries
  Anglo-Saxon 85, 87, 88
mission movement
  Celtic 88, 93
  Celtic/Anglo-Saxon 110
missions
  Anglo-Saxon 84, 88, 113
  Celtic/Anglo-Saxon 122
monasteries, cenobitic 93
monastic 110
  life 70
  models 107
  settlement 79
monasticism 90, 92, 93, 95, 109, 110, 122
  Celtic 88, 93, 94, 97
  cenobitic 94
  early Egyptian 41
  Egyptian 110
  eremitic 93, 94
  missional 95, 122
monastics 118
monks, eremitic 95
Monophysitism 53

N

Nestorianism 42, 53
Nestorius 42
Nicea, Council of 63
Nobatia. *See* Nubia
north Africa 62
Nubia 52, 53

O

obedience 95, 109, 113, 124
Origen 21–23, 117
Ostrogoths. *See* Goths

P

pagan temples, destruction 87
Palestine 93, 110
Pantaenus 21
Patrick, Saint 78, 87, 88, 123
Paul (the apostle) 92, 97, 106, 108, 124
peregrinus 84, 86, 97
persecuted 120
persecution 21, 42, 43, 119, 121
Persia 35, 41–43, 93, 110, 120, 123, 124
pilgrim 70, 84–86, 88, 123, 124
pilgrim-preachers 124
Polycarp 21, 107
prayer 88, 93–96, 104–106, 109, 110, 116, 120, 124
preaching 20–22, 84, 86, 93, 113, 116, 122, 123

R

Radbod 86
reconciliation 92, 120
reign of Christ 88, 91, 92, 108, 109, 117
Remigius, Bishop 69
royal priesthood 103, 105, 120

S

shrine-smashing 23
Simeon Stylites 110
Slavs 123
Sons and Daughters of the Covenant 41, 93, 109, 116
soteriology 115
Spain 62
spiritual warfare 95, 116, 118
Syria 35, 42, 88, 93, 110, 123

T

temple-smashing 23–26
temple-torching 23
Tertullian 22, 104, 106, 108, 118, 121
Theodore of Mopsuestia 42
Theophilus, bishop of Gothia 63
translating Scripture 43

U

Ulfilas, Bishop 63

V

Vandals 62
violence. *See* temple-smashing
Visigoths. *See* Goths
Vladimir (prince of Kievan Rus) 121

W

Wictbert 84
Wilfrid of Hexham 84, 85
Willibald 86
Willibrord 84–87, 123
worship 25, 26, 70, 90–96, 98, 104–107, 109, 115, 117–120, 125
worshiping communities 97, 98, 119, 120
Wulfilas. *See* Ulfilas

Visit us at missionbooks.org

Through God's Eyes
A Bible Study of God's Motivations for Missions

Patrick O. Cate | Paperback & ePub

This revised classic workbook features updated resources to help readers better understand the needs and growth of missions today. It also includes revised questions and suggestions for further reading for deeper reflection and understanding. *Through God's Eyes* is an invaluable resource for those seeking to investigate God's passion for His world. This study guide is designed to bring us into the Word personally, help us discover inductively what God is saying, and gain a better sense of His direction for our lives. *Through God's Eyes* can function as a personal Bible study, or as part of an introduction to missions or a biblical theology of missions course for a small group, Sunday school, college or seminary class.

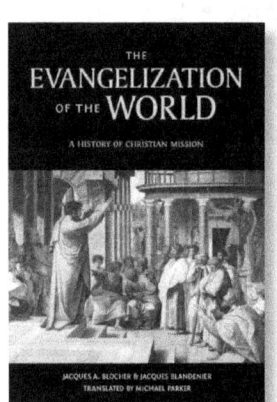

The Evangelization of the World
A History of Christian Mission

Jacques A. Blocher, Jacques Blandenier (Authors), Michael Parker (Translator) | Paperback only

Written in an engaging style and intended largely for a lay audience, *The Evangelization of the World* tells the remarkable story of how Christianity grew from an insignificant Jewish sect in the first century until, by the beginning of the twenty-first century, it had become the world's first truly global religion. The book is careful to explain historical context and mission theory, but the foci of the narrative are the great personalities of mission— the Apostle Paul, St. Martin of Tours, St. Patrick, St. Francis Xavier, John Eliot, Count Von Zinzendorf, William Carey, Robert Morrison, David Livingstone, Mary Slessor, Albert Schweitzer, and many others—who make this account of the expansion of the church a fascinating and often dramatic tale. In addition, the book does not neglect the great mission conferences of the twentieth century, nor does it avoid the controversial aspects of mission that, in many instances, continue to vex the movement today.

Available at missionbooks.org

www.ingramcontent.com/pod-product-compliance
Lightning Source LLC
Chambersburg PA
CBHW071245070526
44583CB00017B/2337